THE CENTURY COMPANION TO

THE WINES OF

BURGUNDY

GRAHAM CHIDGEY

D0278102

CENTURY PUBLISHING

LONDON

Also in this series

The Century Companion to Whiskies *Derek Cooper*
The Century Companion to Cognac and Other Brandies *James Long*
The Century Companion to the Wines of Spain and Portugal
Jan Read
The Century Companion to the Wines of Bordeaux
Pamela Vandyke Price
The Century Companion to the Wines of Champagne
Pamela Vandyke Price

Series Editor Pamela Vandyke Price

Copyright © Graham Chidgey 1977, 1984

First published in Great Britain in 1977 by
Pitman Publishing Ltd
Revised edition published in 1984 by
Century Publishing Co. Ltd,
Portland House
12–13 Greek Street, London W1V 5LE

ISBN 0 7126 0404 9

Printed in Great Britain in 1984 by
Hazell Watson & Viney Limited,
Member of the BPCC Group,
Aylesbury, Bucks

To my friends in Burgundy for their friendship

Acknowledgements

In producing this revised edition, seven years after the first, I have needed to reappraise my feelings and some of my stated facts on Burgundy wines. As with the original version, I remain indebted to Pamela Vandyke Price, the series editor, for her encouragement and commonsense approach.

All the authors listed in the Further Reading have been referred to at length, and I am fortunate in my knowledgeable predecessors.

A great deal of my information has been gained, and my opinions born, in the company of Pierre Maufoux of Santenay, a shipper who is a master in the art of bringing out the best character in Burgundy wines. My thanks to him and to Danièle Maufoux for their hospitality over the last fifteen years and for the delightful opportunity I have been given to learn of Burgundy in a traditional family atmosphere could not be greater.

Because this book is required as an information source both for the traveller and for the non-travelling student of Burgundy wines, it has unfortunately been necessary to omit all the wines of the Beaujolais and Mâconnais (southern Burgundy). Available space does not allow sufficient pages to cover a fascinating, beautiful and, to me, a favourite region. I hope another writer will be given the chance in this series to remedy this omission in the same outspoken style as the glowing charms of Beaujolais wines deserve.

Thanks also to the new publisher, Century, for deciding on a revised edition. It causes me, as a wine shipper, to think once again of Burgundy wines as they might appear to the uninitiated, and I hope that my admiration yet gentle criticism of Burgundy wines will not go unnoticed by consumer and producer.

Graham Chidgey 1984

Contents

Foreword   vi
1   Burgundy – the Wine Trade   1
2   The History   14
3   How Burgundy is Made   26
4   Bottles, Labels and Buying   50
5   Burgundy Wine Journey   62
6   The Food of Burgundy   113

APPENDICES

1   Wine Tasting – by Pamela Vandyke Price   118
2   Glossary of Wine Terms   128
3   Further Reading   132
4   Appellation Contrôlée in Burgundy   133
    Index   143

Maps

The Wine Regions of Burgundy   viii
The Burgundy Region – Dijon/Beaune   63
The Burgundy Region – Beaune/Chalon-sur-Saône   64
Chablis   67

Foreword

Writers of many of the books dealing with wine for the benefit of both the drinker and the traveller tend to be somewhat dogmatic about what the wines are like. To give a single sentence of generalisation about any one wine risks puzzling the reader, whose experiences of trying these particular wines may have resulted in his forming a totally contrary opinion. On the other hand too *much* detail about the wines of a fairly small region can be bewildering.

There is no one way to overcome this difficulty. I know that some people visiting a wine region, or studying wines, like to have definite guidelines as to the general character of the wines of a particular village. Others prefer to try and form their own opinions. Yet, if you have only a short time available when travelling, you may never encounter an absolutely typical wine and may leave wondering why I should have described it in a particular way. The same applies to explorations in fine wines on any list. My only hope is that no lover of wine will be put off by one disappointment, any more than he will be foolish enough to form a fixed opinion of a wine as the result of one single fortunate experience. Fine Burgundy is a minority group in the world of wine and therefore I think that dogmatic assertions of quality are valueless – indeed, unwise.

Since the first edition of this book was published in 1977 there has been one major book on Burgundy, written by Anthony Hanson, M.W., (published by Faber in 1982) that conspicuously asserts some strongly held opinions, most of which are not at all flattering to the integrity of the Burgundy wine trade. Indeed, Hanson offers the amateur the first opportunity to read openly about the methods used by growers and shippers to enliven (into drinkable, attractive wines) the modest wines that are made in poor vintages. Some of their practices are definitely outside the law (ie blending with other non-Burgundy wines) and resorted to only by the less reputable people. Some of the other methods, such as degrees of *chaptalisation* and of pasteurisation are matters of opinion, decided by individuals.

The faults of the Burgundy trade are known to all occupied in the business. The wisest reaction of the public is not to buy any Burgundy just for the fashion of the names on its label, nor to continue to buy any Burgundy that fails to provide a decent rapport of quality with price. The future of Burgundy lies, and must always lie, in the greater production of quality wines.

So – take nothing for granted in Burgundy. Just because the name on a label is well known, being that of a sought-after and much publicised village or vineyard, don't automatically assume that the wine will be a great one. Just because a shipper has established the name of his house in the minds of a particular public, don't think that you, personally, will always find every single one of his wines to your liking, or even in line with the standards of quality you yourself form after a little experience. But don't, either, reject the chance to try a wine because you have not heard of the name or the shipper.

Try many different wines from different shippers. Find a wine merchant who shares your love of Burgundy and who will frankly admire even the wines of his competitors when these are good. Ideally, get to know your main Burgundy merchant. If this is difficult, at least make contact with him by letter or even by telephone. Report your experiences – this will help him to know the sort of wines you need and enjoy.

lists and in some books, it is fair to think of them as quite separate. In addition to the difference in the regions, different grape varieties are used and different traditions of winemaking are followed, resulting in completely different wines. The Beaujolais and the surrounding regions deserve to be and should be considered quite apart from the more aristocratic wines of Burgundy itself.

CHABLIS

Chablis is a small town and a small wine region much nearer to the southern end of the Champagne district than it is to the Burgundy heart in the Côte d'Or, centred on Beaune. Indeed, the fringe vineyards of Champagne are only 24 kilometres (15 miles) from Chablis, whilst the Côte d'Or is some 104 kilometres (65 miles) further down the autoroute. The Chablis region, 16 kilometres (10 miles) long and 6.4 kilometres (4 miles) wide, running roughly north to south, has been aptly described as an *île vineuse* (wine island).

It produces exclusively dry white wines of varying qualities, from the grandest, with their uniquely chalky flavour, down to the refreshing carafe wines sold by the *pichet* (small jug) in local restaurants.

The town of Chablis is locally called 'Burgundy's golden gate', but it is quiet and unpretentious. The dumpy stone houses seem to have settled into the ground for centuries and, unless you know, you would never suspect that beneath your feet as you walk the streets lie the treasures of pale gold in the Chablis casks known as the *Feuillette* – the stocks of wines.

The whole Chablis vineyard was very much larger in former times. It also seems to have suffered more than other vineyard regions from climatic disasters and diseases. As recently as 1956 a severe frost destroyed so many vines that it was said in Chablis that at least twenty years must pass before production could really recover. Frozen vines had to be cleared out and the vineyards had to lie fallow to recover. Planting new vineyards after clearing the ground is costly and the young vines require time to develop and produce. Another three years must pass before the wine can bear an *appellation*. The past twenty years have brought the additional problem of finding labour to work in the vineyards.

THE CÔTE D'OR

Because constant references will be made to the Côte d'Or it is important to realise exactly what this 'golden slope' now is.

The Côte d'Or comprises the two *côtes* (slopes) which are internationally famous: the Côte de Nuits, the centre of which is Nuits St. Georges, and the Côte de Beaune, the centre of which is Beaune. The Côte Chalonnaise immediately to the south of the Côte de Beaune is not, traditionally, within the Côte d'Or, although the wines of this region are usually listed among those of the Côte d'Or for convenience. To divide up the different Burgundy wine regions too much can make for confusion, although the wines do differ greatly in style.

The vineyards of the Côte d'Or extend for 64 kilometres (40 miles) and the area is well named 'golden'. The colour patterns during harvest time and just after, when the leaves of the vines turn a brilliant red and gold, are spectacular and it is a pity that more visitors do not see this region after the vintage.

It is important to remember the two distinct areas that, together, make up the Côte d'Or, because the wines from each are in fact very different. Many readers of this book may already possess a fair knowledge of wine, but there may be others who, for the first time, are developing an interest and who are trying to widen their knowledge. As there is always more to be learned for every one of us when we tackle wine, I am venturing to restate certain basics, which may be of help to both visitors and students who want to find out a bit more about the great classic wines and where they come from. First, it is important to be clear about what may be called the geographical skeleton of the Burgundy wine area. This really will add to future enjoyment of the wine, so study a map and then the subdivisions that I am dealing with here will not seem complicated.

THE CÔTE DE NUITS

The Côte de Nuits begins a few miles to the south of Dijon at Fixin, though the village of Chenôve, with its ancient winepress, is the last remaining village to the north of this *côte* and is now actually in the suburbs of Dijon, where wine is still made. In former times there was an area in the Côte de Dijon too, but this began to fall into desuetude after the phylloxera plague of the late nineteenth century and with the expansion of Dijon in the industrial era. Vines were also once grown to the north of Dijon, but these have now disappeared, so the Côte de Dijon can be dismissed as something of the past. From Fixin down to Corgoloin and Comblanchien, with its marble quarry, is the area known as the Côte de Nuits, with Nuits St. Georges as its main town and centre. Between the two limits of this *côte* lie the world's most famous and valuable vineyards – although a partisan of Bordeaux might challenge this statement!

The slope is a concentrated, narrow strip of land about 19.2 kilometres (12 miles) long, running almost due north-south, with the vineyards planted on rising ground up the hillside and finishing only when the soil gives way to the wooded hilltops. The vines face south-east; from this position they receive the sunshine, which continues from early morning to early evening, without the grapes risking being scorched by any great heat from the sun's rays. The hillside includes a succession of villages, between which there are many coombs and crevices; these break up the vineyards with changes of soil that are quite noticeable to the eye. Vines planted on the flat, the soil of which is reddish clay, alongside the road (RN74) contrast with those planted higher up the hillsides where pebbles and stones predominate in the topsoil and a paler tone is seen. The wines made here are almost entirely red. They have certain characteristics in common which are probably easier to distinguish when you know something of the significance of their names – many of them as romantic-sounding as that of the Côte de Nuits itself.

Not all Côte de Nuits wines are great and fine – this is impossible from a mere 1,600 hectares (3,953 acres) of vines, with several hundred growers responsible for vinification, albeit within the relevant laws. There is much individuality of practice in both owners and makers (see page 26), but the great and fine wines *are* to be found in this area even if you cannot often afford them.

It is fair to say that in the Côte de Nuits certain anxieties are now spreading through the wine trade. The total production of the Côte de Nuits wines is much smaller than that of the Côte de Beaune, the resulting demand quite often exceeding supply. When the growers' products are easy to sell there is a natural decline in attention to detail, which has begun to show in certain vintages. This may largely be due to the sharp increase in tourism, which has brought many willing buyers into direct contact with the producer, for 'cellar door' sales to Parisians and others staying in the region over a weekend who like to think that they are effecting a saving by making their wine purchases in this way. In addition currency restrictions limiting foreign travel have caused the French to concentrate on exploring their own country. Anyway, it is now estimated that 39 per cent of all Côte de Nuits wines are sold by the grower direct to the consumer. Inevitably there has been some aggravation caused by this new trend and I must digress to dissuade anyone in the U.K. and U.S.A. from wishing to join this buying craze. Leave the job of buying Burgundy to your merchant! You may pay less and get more – in terms of quality – in the end than if you take a chance and back your own judgement on the spot.

It is also alleged that some Côte de Nuits wines are beginning to suffer from the over-fertilisation of the vineyards, which has been used to force up production. My experience is not extensive enough to assess the truth of this but it is evident that the colour in these wines seems to be less than it once was. Too many of the wines are lacking in body and, often, they do not have the richness and generous character or the exceptional finesse found in the best examples. Nevertheless, readers will find many Côte de Nuits wines which show why they have gained their reputation: note the expansive bouquet, the elegance of the fruit flavours and the depth of taste that fills the mouth of the fortunate drinker.

THE CÔTE DE BEAUNE

This starts immediately at Ladoix Serrigny and extends south to Dézize, just past Santenay. The main RN74 road running virtually parallel with the slopes of the Côte d'Or, now fortunately carries less traffic because the motorway takes the heavy lorries.

There is an immediate visible difference between the Côte de Nuits and the Côte de Beaune because the hillsides of the Côte de Nuits are nearer to the main road and much steeper. It is certainly noticeable that the soil on each side of the road here is very different: on the east side it is darker, thicker in texture, more obviously earthy and, indeed, more as you would expect in a flat, rather low-lying plot. This whole area leads down into the River Saône, which in prehistoric times was a vast inland lake – worth remembering, because the fossils of such places enrich the soil, especially for vines. It is not difficult to understand that the best wines come only from the slopes between the old road and the hillside or *côte* itself, the finest growths being concentrated in the positions on the middle slope. Here they are slightly sheltered and receive the contributory elements of sun, rain and advantageous drainage, in addition to enjoying soil better suited to vines. Consequently, the vineyard area of the slope is not wide – 3.2 kilometres (2 miles) at its widest, as little as 640 metres (700 yards) at its narrowest.

THE CÔTE CHALONNAISE

The Côte Chalonnaise is, geographically, an extension of the Côte de Beaune and therefore the Côte d'Or and takes its name from the nearby town of Chalon-sur-Saône. The same grape varieties are required according to *Appellation Contrôlée* regulations and the four village *Appellations* of the Côte Chalonnaise – Mercurey, Montagny, Rully and Givry – are now becoming familiar to those who look at the lists of wine merchants, seeking a Burgundy that their modest budgets will not find too taxing. Mercurey is perhaps the leader of the wines and several maps and writers now refer to the '*Région de Mercurey*' as a group title as distinct from the Côte Chalonnaise.

The recent increased popularity of the wines from the

specialist member of the firm and they will have cellars available in the villages of their interest. The small family grower, however, will probably own just one cellar, this being either adjacent to his house or nearby in his village and this is where all the grapes will be brought at harvest time.

Grapes from within the same *Appellation Contrôlée* region may be pressed and fermented together, but of course grapes from individual vineyards and different *Appellations* are kept separate by law. Therefore, within a cellar there may be several different wines for A.O.C. (*Appellation d'Origine Contrôlée*) purposes.

This is the main reason why Burgundies that are entitled to be labelled '*Mise du domaine*' ('*domaine* bottled') are not actually bottled in the vineyard where the grapes are grown (unless this happens to coincide with the location of the owner's cellar), but in the proprietor's cellars, which may be in a quite different, and possibly even fairly distant, village. For example, a Volnay may be labelled as '*domaine* bottled' when the *domaine* where it is bottled is in fact at Pommard; the wine has been made at this *domaine* and the description is therefore correct.

Underground cellar for storing young wines in casks

THE IMPORTANCE OF ÉLÉVAGE AND BOTTLING

Until the early 1970s most Burgundy was shipped from Beaune or Nuits St. Georges, these being the two commercial towns of the Côte d'Or, in oak hogsheads, each approximately representing twenty-four dozen bottles when bottled. The U.K., Belgium, Holland, Denmark, West Germany and, to a lesser extent, Switzerland, were permitted to import in bulk, though the U.S.A. always shipped Burgundy in bottle. The quality of bottling in these foreign lands would vary enormously, which led to abuse, some of the wines being blended, either to change their style or to stretch the purchase for financial gain. Fortunately this is now all past history. The lead given by the U.S.A. for Burgundies being bottled by their *négociants* (shippers) or by the individual *domaines* has brought the genuine flavour of the Pinot Noir grape (for red wines), and the Chardonnay grape (for white wines), into familiar recognition by the Burgundy drinkers of the countries formerly suffering from large quantities of blended Burgundy.

Consequently, the Burgundy shippers have needed to enlarge their cellars, equipment and staff to cope with the demands of storing more wines in bottle. As Burgundy is a temperamental wine when resting in its oak barrels, the quality of bottling at a technical level cannot be sufficiently stressed. The many shipping firms of international distinction have paid worthwhile attention to their bottling conditions.

In the last two decades there has grown a vogue for *domaine* bottling for certain markets and customers, the theory being that the grower who has matured his own wine and then undertaken the bottling for his own label must, by definition, produce a superior wine to that of a *négociant*. In fact, there is no such guarantee logically associated with a *domaine*-bottled wine. Some *domaines* care for and bottle their wines extremely well – others do not.

Domaines in general are small and generally need much more expensive equipment than they can afford. Technical knowledge of the upbringing of young wines has not been a noted feature of Burgundy, as the older *vigneron* or grower was not brought up to realise the need for this expertise. It must be admitted that the younger generation of *vignerons* is much better educated in the techniques of winemaking and less conservative than the older generation; nonetheless, the rush to *domaine* bottling just to follow a fashion did produce some erratic, very questionable qualities as well as some fine wines.

Remember that *domaines* or estates cannot buy in wines, even from the same A.O.C.s, to help with a blend, so that if a *domaine* in, say, Volnay, has made a wine somewhat lacking in fruit but well appointed with tannin its owner cannot buy from his neighbour another Volnay registering greater fruitiness in order to blend into a better balanced wine. A *domaine* must make the best of the wine it produces.

Not always will a *domaine* be excellent at the three essential stages of wine-producing –

1   Farming the vineyards to produce the best results the soil and weather permit.

2   *'Élévage'*: care of the wine during its development in wooden barrels.
3   Bottling under healthy conditions at the right time and taking all reasonable precautions against the dangers of bottling before full analysis has been taken to prevent later upsets in bottle.

When *domaine* bottling is bad, it is very bad, but the *négociant* who does the bottling may also have faults. It is prudent, therefore, to analyse any Burgundy before it is bottled, primarily to check that the wine really has finished its malo-lactic fermentation and that this is not still dormant in the wine. Often bottlers do not check this and, later on, after the wine has gone into bottle, it starts 'working' or fermenting again – something that can be detected by the presence of minuscule bubbles at the edge of the wine in the glass and a slightly 'prickly' sensation that will be noted on the tongue. This malo-lactic fermentation is something that lasts only for a short time – possibly only a few days – and is quite normal in the wine's development, but the wine must get through this stage before it is bottled, otherwise it will never be quite right.

As in all walks of life, decisions are dictated by ambitions, standards and practical considerations and Burgundy is no different. Some *domaines* have perfected the three stages of winemaking previously outlined and some *négociants* have succeeded in successive generations in building a reputation for outstanding skill in buying, blending and presenting their Burgundy wines to a regularly high quality. Both these sections of Burgundy life need each other to create a healthy rivalry. Sadly beneath the few at the top there are many *domaines* and *négociants* who fall short in their abilities.

Hopefully no lover of Burgundy will ever make a dogmatic assessment based solely on the label evidence of a *domaine* wine against that of a *négociant*. Judge all Burgundy on the quality you find inside the bottle.

Something that very much affects the wine-loving traveller in Burgundy is that, as a result of the increased popularity of *domaine* bottling, *domaine*-bottled wines may be offered for sale to the holidaymaker at very fancy prices; the trade buyer will be more alert to the quality of wines offered in this way but the tourist may get something that is both expensive and of poor quality. On a recent visit I paid to Pommard I noted that one grower, who would have sold his ordinary Bourgogne Rouge to me at a fairly modest price, was charging nearly three times as much for exactly the same wine to those who hope to purchase something *'domaine*-bottled at the *domaine'*.

Domaine-bottled Burgundies are usually purchased by the

importing shippers of the U.K., U.S. and other export markets either on a direct agency basis or through a *courtier* (see below). The disadvantage of buying as an established agent is that a buyer is tied to a *domaine* or even to a *négociant*, whatever the vintage may have produced. Therefore selection can only be made on a limited basis – those wines available through one particular concern.

Because of the complexity of style, variety and quality of wines produced under a single A.O.C. (take Meursault as an example), it would be very restricting for, say, a London merchant to offer only the wines of one single grower or one particular *négociant*. Those wine drinkers who recognise the fluctuating qualities of Burgundy should therefore try to buy their wines from a merchant who knows the regions within this overall vineyard and travels extensively in the area so as to be able to taste and buy independently.

However, the increase in *domaine* bottling has caused some shippers in Burgundy to make deals with vineyard owners, either agreeing to do the distribution of the wine for them or to buy the whole of the crop – an obvious advantage as far as the small proprietor is concerned. So, if the *vigneron* (grower) does not bottle his own wine, he has to find a buyer among the shippers.

THE *COURTIER* AND THE *COMMISSIONAIRE EN VINS*

The way the grower proceeds is to make use of a *courtier de campagne* (broker). The *courtier* will earn a commission of 2 per cent from the *négociant* on what he arranges for the *vigneron* to sell, and, if he can, he takes another 2 per cent from the *vigneron* as well; he lives solely by his commissions and does not hold stocks of wine. *Courtiers* are usually highly specialised dealers in wine, knowing exactly the various wines of different villages and cultivating a working relationship with the growers as well as the shippers. They can save the shippers a great deal of time because of their ability, as it were, to pre-select the stocks that they know a particular shipper will want to buy.

If a well-established *courtier* does acquire some stock of wines, he is known as a *commissionnaire en vins*. But he will not hold this stock in his own cellars. He will keep it – usually only for a short time – in the cellars of the grower and he will sell it as soon as possible, charging a commission of about 5 per cent.

SHIPPERS AND AGENTS

The *négociant* who may also have a business, either as shipper and/or merchant in an export market (see page 53), will have large cellars, in which the wines he has bought may be stored for maturation and eventually bottled. Many of these cellars are open to visitors and a guided tour of at least one is essential for the lover of Burgundy.

The *négociant*'s job consists of supplying the wine merchants who buy from him and selling the wines he holds – either under his own label or labelled for the purchaser. Obviously, substantial stocks of wine are essential for the *négociant* to maintain continuity of his particular 'house style' over a range of wines; quantities are often required far in excess of those village wines that the *négociant* has been able to buy himself direct from individual growers. The buyer of the establishment will therefore buy in various lots from the required A.O.C.s, and the wines will be blended in the cellars of the shipper. This process, known as *assemblage*, is a skilled task, requiring much experience, in order that the shipper can maintain the house style that he has found popular with his customers. The retail merchant who will buy the wines (or the restaurant, hotel chain, or similar organisation) will also know the wine his clientèle prefers.

This is why the name of the house is of such importance when choosing Burgundy – the wines of one establishment may be perfectly good but quite unlike those of another, which are equally good. And continuity is something of which the purchaser must be assured: obviously, no customer wants to select and ship, for example, a light, fruity Beaune only to find that, when he re-orders that wine (having found that his public like it as much as he does) that it, albeit selling under the same name, is now a fat, overweight type of Beaune. This is why style control is so important and why certain styles have, over the years, become associated with certain establishments.

Some *négociants*, in times of prosperity, bought vineyards for themselves. For example, in the A.O.C. Beaune area, there are more shippers owning vineyards than *vignerons*; Chanson Père et Fils, Bouchard Père et Fils, Joseph Drouhin, Louis Latour and Jaboulet Vercherre are all substantial proprietors.

It would be impossible for a Burgundy shipper to cover all the export markets with which he deals from Burgundy itself: even if, physically, he had the staff to do so, the expense involved would make the ultimate price of the wine even higher. So he often appoints an agent or distributor in each of his main markets.

This agent may sometimes be one person, but usually consists of a firm experienced in that market, who will be handling other wines, but of course not those that are in direct competition with those of the shipper. Rather confusingly, such a firm, if it deals with supplying the wine trade rather than doing business directly with the public, is also known in the U.K. as a 'shipper'; but the firm may, in a few instances, be doing business as a merchant as well, and have arranged an exclusivity for the wines of a particular Burgundy house, which sell these within a specific area.

There are also the big shippers who own retail chains, off-licences and hotels and restaurant groups, as well as controlling public houses. The smaller firms, which may enjoy outstanding prestige, can be equally important, especially as regards certain wines that are never available in vast quantities because only small amounts are made. This is why you may see the name of a particular Burgundy shipper in a number of different places even in the U.K. – the establishment has arranged to sell the way that seems most strategically effective, and immediately profitable.

Some U.K. agents for the main Burgundy houses may have been associated with the establishments they represent for generations, or they may now be creating a new market for a particular house.

2

The History

The hill formation of the ridge that is today known as the Côte d'Or, the heart of the Burgundy wine country, was created during the Jurassic period, 150 million years ago. Archaeologists have found traces of man living there 12,000 years B.C., when horses were driven up to and off the rock of Solutré to perish on the cliffs below and serve as fodder for humans. Works of art dating from the sixth century B.C. were found in 1952 at Châtillon-sur-Seine and, in the Bronze Age, what is now part of Burgundy was crossed by trading tracks that made it known as 'the highway of tin and amber'.

Caesar conquered Gaul and the tribes of the region of Burgundy in 52 B.C. and subsequently Roman civilisation extended widely in the area. The actual name 'Burgundia', however, is first noted about A.D. 500 and refers to the fair-skinned warriors from Germany who took over the region after Roman power declined.

In the latter part of the fourth century both the Franks and the Burgundians became Christian – at this time the area belonged to France. Later, in the eighth century, under Charlemagne (who interested himself seriously in wine growing), the region became increasingly prosperous due to the richness of the land as well as its strategic importance. One of Charlemagne's ordinances forbade the treading of grapes by foot as, even then, it was considered unhygienic. His name is remembered over the centuries for his vineyard holding in Corton and is commemorated in the white wine Corton Charlemagne. However, after Charlemagne's death in 814 the region was divided and Burgundy became a duchy at the beginning of the eleventh century.

The Middle Ages

Burgundy was of enormous importance in the Middle Ages, both because of its powerful dukes and on account of the growing power of the religious orders in the region. As early as the sixth century A.D. there is a record of a piece of land in the Dijon region being donated by the then King of Burgundy, Gontram, to form the Abbey of St. Benigne. From this time onwards families who were granted noble status made many gifts to the Church of vineyards or properties where vines could be cultivated. Many nobles themselves also owned wine-producing estates, but the dominating influence in the evolution of Burgundy wine was certainly the Church. The great churches and abbeys of Burgundy are witness to the prosperity and importance of the religious orders. The mighty foundation of Cluny, established in the tenth century by a pious Duke of Aquitaine, was so powerful through its chain of other houses that its abbot often exercised more authority even than the Pope. The Cluniac monks acted through their daughter abbeys, being, in Sir Stephen Runciman's words, 'the American Express of the Middle Ages'; they ran hostels for pilgrims and travellers and pursued scholarly research of all kinds, as well as being possibly the supreme exponents of the sacred liturgy. Throughout Europe they influenced politics as well as learning.

In 1098 three Cluniac monks, including an Englishman, Stephen Hardy, set up a separate establishment at Cîteaux – so called because it was in a low-lying, marshy place, among the reeds, *cistels*. Here they revived the austerity and discipline of earlier monastic traditions. St. Bernard, who preached the Third Crusade in Burgundy, came to Cîteaux in 1112 and encouraged this reforming spirit by founding the Abbey of Clairvaux. In addition, the Cistercians, as they were now called, became renowned as wine producers, showing how poor soil, fit for nothing else, could be cultivated to produce remarkable wine. They established a branch of their order at what is now Clos de Vougeot – its shape and style are typically Cistercian – and in 1141 the nuns of the Cistercian Abbey of Notre Dame du Tart purchased a vineyard in Morey, which remained in their possession until the French Revolution. This vineyard, the world-famous Clos de Tart, has never been split up between owners and now belongs in its entirety to the well-known shipper, Mommessin of Mâcon.

Golden Age

The 'Golden Age' of the Duchy of Burgundy was the fourteenth century, after Philippe le Hardi, fourth son of the King of France, became Duke of Burgundy on the death of his father. He was succeeded by Jean Sans Peur, Philippe le Bon, and Charles le Téméraire, and the period between 1364 and 1477 was a brilliant one as regards works of art, economic and political achievements and extravagantly lavish entertainments and social life. The Duchy was enormously powerful, its dukes ruling the entire Netherlands and also Artois, Picardy, Luxemburg and Franche-Comté, in addition to Burgundy itself. Even the King of France was in awe of the Duke of Burgundy, whose forces were of prime importance in any war. (Remember that, until 1353, the English crown owned the south-west of France and the English thought they had a right to even more of the country.)

The French court drank the wines of Burgundy, both for reasons of diplomacy and of proximity. (The English drank Bordeaux for the same reasons.) Philippe le Bon, on his marriage to Isabella of Portugal in 1429, created the chivalric order of the Toison d'Or, or Golden Fleece, one of the most influential brotherhoods of its kind, which still exists to this day. The magnificence of life at the Burgundy court was remarkable. In 1430, at a banquet in honour of the new duchess, a gigantic pie was presented; this held a giant live sheep, its fleece painted blue and its horns gold. Accounts of the ducal catering are extraordinary: the chief pantler or steward had fifty esquires under him just to serve the meals. Go into the courtyard of the Hospices de Beaune, built by the Chancellor with Flemish workmen, and appreciate the wealth that made this building possible.

Burgundy was again joined to the French crown in the fifteenth century, but its boundaries were extended and its governors were still men of great importance who, being concerned with protecting the Duchy's frontiers, were still in a position to maintain a type of independence. This lasted until the outbreak of the French Revolution at the end of the eighteenth century. In the wars against Napoleon I, the Austrians invaded Burgundy and occupied it after the Battle of Waterloo in 1815. In the Franco-Prussian War, 1870–71, the French were victorious at the Battle of Nuits in 1870 and again at Dijon in 1871; this is why the Cross of the Légion d'Honneur is seen in the arms of Dijon today.

War – and Peace

In World War I Burgundy was not subjected to actual fighting, but in World War II, the region had to endure the advance of the Allied forces coming up from the south and fierce fighting during the withdrawal of the occupying Germans; great tales are told of how stocks of fine wines were hidden during the occupation so as not to be looted. One would-be clever producer sank his in a pond, but to his horror the labels came unstuck and floated off and the Germans recovered the bottles.

Wynford Vaughan Thomas, then a liaison officer between the British, American and French forces, relates how, in the final stages of the war, the French general in command had halted just below Beaune, in a dilemma as to whether his duty really impelled him to launch his troops over what were the finest slopes of the Côte; the British and Americans couldn't understand his delaying. All at H.Q. were sunk in doubt and despair when suddenly a motor-cyclist arrived, breathless, and flung himself into the C.O.'s presence with a cry: 'Mon

Général, the Germans are only occupying the inferior slopes!'
The general leapt to his feet with a roar. *'J'attaque!'* he
cried – and did.

Today, in spite of the building of autoroutes and radical
changes in vine growing and wine making, Burgundy is
prosperous (some might say almost spoiled) and maintains
much of its traditional character. The attraction of this region
now probably lies in the fact that it is essentially a country
region, even its largest towns never wholly cutting one off from
the winding lanes, fat pastures and dumpy grey stone houses
among fields, plantations of trees and, never far away, the
vineyards. It is a countryman's country and its wines are the
wines of those who have a direct and wholehearted ability to
enjoy life. Little wonder that so many of us love it so much!

Wine Fraternities and Feasts

CONFRÈRIE DES CHEVALIERS DU TASTEVIN

This is one of the most famous – Burgundians would say the
most famous – wine orders in the world. In some regions in
France the wine orders grew out of the medieval fraternities
which supervised the particular trade of the area. Holding
reunions and banquets, these fraternities publicised the wines,
at the same time often acting in a benevolent role on behalf of
both members of the fraternity and their families. The resusci-
tation and creation of such fraternities has been a notable
feature of the promotion of French wines in the later part of the
twentieth century.

One chronicler of the French wine orders says that the
Chevaliers du Tastevin is an order founded on *ésprit* rather than
the continuation of a historic tradition; this term, so difficult to
translate exactly, does in fact sum up the dedication and
sensitivity of the founders, Camille Rodier and Georges
Faiveley. Both of them had been deeply involved in the wine of
the Burgundy area and the countryside of the wine regions in
general in the period between the wars when world trade was
depressed and Burgundy had a succession of poor vintages. The
Confrèrie was founded on 16 November 1934, the organisers
having already invited a number of well-known personalities
both from France and other export markets to take part in the
occasion. The Chevaliers du Tastevin grew slowly but steadily
in number, and in 1944 they bought the building of Clos de
Vougeot, a former Cistercian foundation, and began a serious
programme of restoring the great buildings to their former
impressive state. Most of the funds required then and since
have been donated by various Chapters of the Confrèrie
overseas – notably the U.S.A.

Ceremonial dress of senior Members of Chevaliers du Tastevin at Clos de Vougeot

It is widely believed that membership of the Chevaliers du Tastevin is restricted to members of the wine, restaurant and hotel trades, but this is not the true case, for membership also includes representatives of the arts, commerce and the sciences, on an international level. Joining the order is a sought-after privilege, if only because members qualify for taking part in the regular dinners in the Clos de Vougeot premises – although they pay for the honour. Membership of the Confrèrie – which includes women – does not necessarily mean that the member is an outstanding authority on the wines of Burgundy. Nor are members all wealthy: sensible arrangements are made so that the Confrèrie includes a true cross-section, at least of those from all walks of life in Burgundy itself. There are about twenty meetings each year, when 500–600 people sit down to a gastronomic banquet. The atmosphere of these dinners epitomises France's love of *'les belles choses'* (the good things of life – in other words food and drink).

Extending their authority, the Chevaliers du Tastevin instituted a system of 'wine approval' for Burgundy wines in

1950. Those who wish, whether growers or *négociants*, may present their wine or wines to a special committee, free of charge; the wine will be judged according to its vintage and *Appellation* at a blind tasting – price is not mentioned. If the committee gives its approval, the Chevaliers du Tastevin then sell to the applicant their specially designed labels, each one numbered to the quantity of the bottles officially declared, and only these may bear the particular *Tasteviné* label. To possess this label definitely enhances both the prestige and value of the wine, at least in France, in certain export markets and in many smart restaurants throughout the world: *Tasteviné* wines give the *sommelier* something to add to his sales talk!

Many writers on wine suggest that this scrutiny of samples by the Chevaliers is quite severe; I am sure that this may be so but in my own tasting experience I find that too many borderline cases have been approved. I would prefer to see a strengthening of the quality standards if the ordinary consumer, who may know quite a lot about Burgundy, is to take the *Tasteviné* system seriously. At present only about one in two of the wines presented seems to pass the test but perhaps this is rather generous.

The promotional activities on behalf of Burgundy and its wine achieved by the Chevaliers du Tastevin have been quite outstanding and deserve the applause of all wine lovers. The Chevaliers also assist in bringing colour and spectacle to the celebrations for St. Vincent, patron saint of French wine growers, for on the first Saturday following 22 January, St. Vincent's Day, the Chevaliers du Tastevin visit a selected village in the Côte d'Or (a different one each year) to celebrate the health and continued good fortune of the vine. There is a procession and solemn mass and subsequently, of course, much feasting.

To visit Clos de Vougeot is essential for any visitor to Burgundy. Even a few moments devoted to seeing the original sixteenth-century buildings and gigantic old presses will be an unforgettable souvenir. Guides provide a complete history of the premises (see page 78) and pictures of the ceremonies give some idea, albeit an inadequate one, of the light and colour in the great hall at one of the banquets.

COUSINERIE DE BOURGOGNE

Savigny-lès-Beaune is the home of the Cousinerie, whose aim is to promote the wines of this village slightly more than those of its neighbours. From the sixteenth century there was a Confrèrie de St. Cassien, which only ceased its acitivities at the French Revolution. This fraternity included the people from neighbouring villages and, by the eighteenth century, members congregating in Savigny for the feast of St. Cassien on 5 August had become so numerous that the church had to be extended! The Cousinerie as it exists today was founded in 1960 on the feast of St. Vincent and it holds four *cousinages* each year: on the Sunday before St. Vincent's Day, the first Saturday in April, the first Saturday in June and the third Sunday in November, immediately before the sale of the Hospices de Beaune wines (see page 22). The Cousinerie has gained a reputation for hospitality – its predecessors used to put up visitors in their own houses for the annual jollifications – and unswerving devotion to putting Savigny-lès-Beaune wines on the map; as the area is important for sparkling as well as still wines, these naturally play a part in the annual celebrations.

Information may be obtained from the Secretariat of the Cousinerie de Bourgogne, Mairie de Savigny-lès-Beaune, Côte d'Or.

LES PILIERS CHABLISIENS

This order gets its name from the way in which, in the great abbey of Mont St. Michel, the huge pillars of the crypt, dating from the fifteenth century, hold up the entire gigantic building. The first Grand Master and founder of the Confrèrie decided that this should be the fraternity's name. The order extends the names of its officers and other branches in an architectural way, too – a Master Pillar and several Flying Buttresses compose the Chapter of each Cloister.

Les Piliers Chablisiens were founded in 1952, and they, too, give organised regular ceremonies, the most important being the one held to show the wines of the Yonne at the end of November.

Information may be obtained from the Cave des Piliers, 1 rue Étienne Dolet, Chablis.

CONFRÈRIE DES TROIS CEPS

This order is an offshoot of the Chablis fraternity and was founded in 1965. It particularly celebrates the *fête de St. Bris* on the first Sunday after 11 November and the feast of St. Vincent.

The Chevaliers des Trois Ceps were particularly concerned with rebuilding the establishment of the Cadet Roussell of the nursery rhyme. This states that Cadet Roussell had three parishes: St. Bris, Chitry and Irancy; the Aligoté is cultivated at Chitry and the Pinot Noir at Irancy, making an agreeably varied range of wines for the celebrations.

Information may be obtained from Mairie de St. Bris in the Yonne.

COMITÉ DE BOURGOGNE ET L'ORDRE DES GRANDS DUCS D'OCCIDENT

The activities of the Comité are more specially devoted to the arts of Burgundy, but they do sponsor the *Fête de la Vigne et du Vin* which takes place in Dijon at the beginning of September. Their headquarters is the magnificent twelfth-century establishment at Clairvaux, which was built by the monks of the Abbey of Clairvaux for storing their wines.

Information may be obtained from Cellier de Clairvaux, Boulevard de la Trémouille, 21 Dijon.

Wine and Gastronomic Fairs

Although a list of the wine and gastronomic fairs may help the reader in planning a journey in Burgundy, a warning must be offered: beware of the great crowds that attend these functions and the lengthy tastings of wines that may be of no more than average quality. That said, these events can be great fun in a totally light-hearted way and they provide an insight into French sales methods.

LA FOIRE NATIONALE DES VINS

Held at Mâcon, (Saône-et-Loire) during the spring (the date varies from year to year). There is a wide selection of wines from Burgundy although there are some from most of the other French wine regions too. It's a chance to see the differences between the Burgundian wines from specific areas and growers.

Information may be obtained from the Chambre du Commerce, Mâcon.

LA FOIRE AUX VINS DE TABLE

This is held in the middle of August at Chagny, which is a quiet town just off the old N6, close to the most southern villages of the Côte de Beaune. The fair provides an opportunity to taste all the generic *Appellations* of both red and white Burgundy. An entrance fee is charged, plus tasting tickets.

L'EXPOSITION GÉNÉRALE DES VINS DE BOURGOGNE

This is a two-day tasting, well organised and held just before the sale of the wines of the Hospice de Beaune during the third weekend of November each year. It is mainly a trade affair where the young wines are on show alongside those of older vintages.

Information and arrangements for tickets may be obtained from Le Secrétariat des Associations Viticoles, 20 place Monge, Beaune, Côte d'Or.

FOIRE GASTRONOMIQUE

Held in Dijon in the first two weeks of November, this function
has won a reputation for showing an amazing and tantalising
range of gastronomic delights, together with a fair selection of
the wines of Burgundy for sampling. A trade fair in origin, it
has now been opened to the public on payment of an entrance
fee.

Information may be obtained from Boîte Postale 122, Dijon,
Côte d'Or.

LES TROIS GLORIEUSES

This is the biggest Burgundian party of the year. It brings
together all the elements of the Burgundy wine trade
throughout the world: growers, brokers, *négociants*, merchants,
buyers for huge concerns, those from independent and often
smallish firms, buyers for hotel and restaurant chains, and all
who pride themselves on the wine lists of their establishments.
Indeed, it is almost a pity to write about it for the general public
because, unless you already have a definite invitation from
somebody in the wine trade who can assure you of somewhere
to stay, there will be no hope of finding accommodation within
a hundred miles of Beaune. All hotel rooms are booked from
year to year by the wine trade, private houses stuff visitors into
their guest rooms, and Beaune is crowded to overflowing. The
shops display all the local gastronomic specialities, parties go on
at all hours of the day and night and, it is said, the police have
instructions not to apprehend any who are revelling in the
streets but rather to guide them gently to wherever they can find
rest.

Les Trois Glorieuses are held over the third weekend in
November. On the Saturday of this weekend the cellars of the
Hospices de Beaune (see page 93) are open for those who wish
to taste from the cask the wines of the current vintage that are to
be auctioned the next day. Huge crowds push their way in,
many *tastevin* in hand, but it is a job to get near the casks and
often impossible to avoid spitting the young wine on to the floor
without hitting somebody's foot. On this day two other tastings
are held in Beaune, including a range of young Beaujolais in the
Town Hall. Many of the great establishments organise special
tastings in their own cellars, some charging a small entrance
fee, and many offering visitors the chance of trying bottled
wines from previous years, including some really old
Burgundies.

On the Saturday night the Chevaliers du Tastevin hold a
banquet at Clos de Vougeot. The building is floodlit, visible
from miles around, and the occasion is also one for honouring

various visitors who are to be admitted into this Burgundian wine order – a celebrity, such as an ambassador or other important personage, heads the list of those inducted. The meal

---

Escriteau

Première Assiette
La Roulade de Foie Gras à l'Ancienne
escortée d'un Bourgogne Aligoté frais et gouleyant
des Hautes-Côtes de Nuits

Deuxième Assiette
Les Biscuits de Brochet à la Fagon
humidifiés d'un Chablis Grand Cru 1978 subtil et parfumé
Grenouilles – Tasteviné

Entremets
La Pièce de Porc au Poivre Vert
arrosée d'un Côte de Beaune-Villages 1977 fin et bouqueté

Dorure
Le Poulet Villageoise
accompagné d'un Nuits St. Georges 1973 suave et prenant
Les Didiers Saint-Georges – Hospices de Nuits – Cuvée Cabet

Issue de Table
Les Bons Fromages de Bourgogne et d'Ailleurs
rehaussés d'un Echézeaux 1971 de noble lignée
Tasteviné

Boutehors
L'Escargot en Glace et les Poires Clos de Vougeot
Les Petit Fours
Le Café Noir, le Vieux Marc et la Prunelle de Bourgogne
fort idoinés à stimuler vapeurs subtiles du cerveau

Note that, in this sometimes slightly jokey menu, the word '*Entremets*' is the course in the middle of the two main dishes. This is as it used to be in former times until Louis XIV, who had a very sweet tooth, used to have sweetmeats served in the middle of the meal; he also had a huge appetite and, after the 'between dishes' course, would go on for several more, but the courtiers, imitating the menus of the royal table, couldn't cope with so much food. This is why the sweet course is still entitled '*Entremets*' in French menus – although it comes at the end of the meal. But the member of the kitchen staff in charge of the '*Entremets*' is still the vegetable chef. The snail, so much an emblem of Burgundian gastronomy, gets on to this menu in icy form.

is heralded by fanfares on the hunting horns, huge coiled instruments, traditional in France, quite unlike anything sounded by Britain's John Peel. These ring out in the courtyard in Clos de Vougeot before the banquet. The proceedings in addition to the inductions are enlivened by the Cadet de Bourgogne, a group of singers kept going throughout the many hours of the meal by draughts of wine. At intervals the entire company is invited to join in, singing the '*Ban Bourguignon*', a song that chiefly consists of the syllables '*La, la, la*', the hands being waved above the head meanwhile and clapped at intervals. On the previous page is a typical menu from one of the banquets at Clos de Vougeot.

The whole thing sounds like a gastronomic marathon but, with the speeches, inductions and intermittent songs, it takes four to five hours, so food and wine are spaced out and do not seem overwhelming at the time.

On the Sunday afternoon of Les Trois Glorieuses the auction of the Hospices wines is held. For once, elaborate luncheons given on that day are cut short as hosts and buyers rush off to be present at the start of the sale – and perhaps to get themselves in front of the television or other cameras.

Until 1959 the auction was actually held in the cellars of the Hospices, but in that year, the centenary of the sale, it was decided to hold it in a specially erected building in the market place and it has been conducted there ever since. It is usually very cold and the women wear boots – the chill strikes up from the stones of the floor even though heaters operate overhead. The occasion is social and exciting: television cameras and microphones abound, the press are seated on the platform behind the auctioneers and the auctioneer keeps himself going in what can be a six-, or even eight-hour stint, with the help of a bottle of Meursault kept under the table. The closing of the bidding is done *à la chandelle* – that is, as a taper burns down and goes out. But for this event there are two tapers, standing up in a special holder; the announcement '*deuxième feu*' (second light) speeds up the bids which are gathered by the auctioneer's assistant, parading through the hall. The bidding continues for as long as the taper burns. At the end of the sale of the wines, the *marcs* (see page 48) and the brandies are sold. Traditionally the white wines are auctioned first and a certain amount of publicity is usually given to whoever buys the first lot – after this at least some of the press can take themselves away. Eventually another banquet is held in the evening, in the Bastion de Beaune, right underneath the enormous walls of the original fortifications around the town. Anyone accustomed to the stringent fire regulations of certain cities may well be slightly uneasy as they go down the narrow spiral staircase into the enormous dining area – for there appears to be a remarkable shortage of ways out. But nothing goes wrong, except that the diners get hungry because of course the auctioneer has to stay to the end of what may be a very long sale. The two cellars are a wonderful sight; the food is prepared and served by students of the local hotel schools, elaborately but well presented – remarkably so, when it is remembered that several hundred people have to be coped with in such a confined space.

In years that are definitely 'off' as regards the wines, the auction is not held and the wines that are able to be offered for sale are sold privately. It is sometimes commented that the prices paid for the Hospices wines are artificially high, because buyers are often compelled to go on bidding, on account of this occasion being, in the words of a journalist 'the biggest charity sale in the world'. The fact, too, that the wines are from the Côte de Beaune means that they cannot be wholly representative of all the finest reds of Burgundy, and significantly, it is often a white wine that makes the top price. But it is also fair to say that the sale attracts invaluable publicity to Burgundy and that buyers from all over the world can come and meet and discuss not merely the current vintage but other vintages with their *négociants* and friends. Perhaps the most important thing is that the sort of prices that are paid – which make headlines in the French papers and get quite a lot of column inches in many others, as well as dominating the wine trade press at the time – do indicate the general standard that good Burgundy will have achieved in that one particular year.

On the Monday after the weekend the strong-willed move on to Meursault for the lunch known as 'la Paulée'. The word is a local one, meaning the vintage lunch traditionally given by vineyard proprietors to their workers. In the mid-1930s, the time of world Depression, the Mayor of Meursault decided that, in order to publicise the great white wines of Burgundy, and Burgundy wines in general, he would enlarge the scope of the local custom. So now the Town Hall of Meursault is given over to about 300 growers, shippers, vineyard workers, and such visitors as can be squeezed in. (Once in, it is physically impossible to get out, although I suppose if anyone died they might be passed over the heads of those lunching.)

All those attending the Paulée bring their finest bottles for sharing around the tables. It is a matter of pride that each proprietor or grower should have something really special to show off to his neighbours and this traditional exchanging of bottles is a very happy and heartwarming gesture. Though there may be some personality as guest of honour who may speak in reply to a tribute paid, the Paulée is an occasion of informality and robust cheer.

3

How Burgundy is Made

The method of wine making in Burgundy has always been a keen topic of conversation, both within the region and amongst individuals in the export trade. Discussion of how Burgundy is made – or how it should be made – is lively, usually much more so than in any other great wine region. This is because fashion has often decided the growers as to the style of wine they should make; they are not, in making wine, producing a fine product without any reference as to what their customers want – they have to sell the wine once it is made, and therefore have to be aware of the current fashion which inclines customers to buy. It is important, however, to establish some basics before mentioning methods and variations. Let us start with the grapes of the region.

Varieties of Grapes

The grape varieties used for red wines are: Pinot Noir, which is used for all the Côte d'Or and Côte Chalonnaise wines; and Gamay, the Beaujolais grape, also grown in outlying areas of the Côte d'Or and often blended with the Pinot Noir for making Passe Tout Grains (see page 29).

The white wine grapes are: Chardonnay, used for all the white wines from the Côte d'Or, Côte Chalonnaise and Chablis which are to qualify for vineyard, village and area *Appellations*; and Aligoté which is sold under the grape variety name and is not a regional *Appellation*.

PINOT NOIR

If you walk into the vineyards during July, August and September the ripening bunches of Pinot Noir grapes are closer-knit and smaller in size than you would expect by comparison with other wine grapes. This tight bunching can cause rot during either wet or humid weather and the risk of these hazards is only compensated for by the elegance and finesse of the wine made from Pinot Noir. This grape has now long been established as the only variety for red wines capable of maintaining this particularly fine concentration of flavour to the exclusion of all other varieties in Burgundy.

As fine wines rarely appear in abundance, so it is with the production capabilities of the Pinot Noir. It gives a relatively modest yield from the grape villages of the Côte de Nuits and the Côte de Beaune, where the permitted quantity level to be vintaged (or *rendement* as it is termed in French), is 35 hectolitres per hectare (2.4 acres). Increases can be applied for and in particularly fruitful years will be granted, although usually this increase takes place in vintages where, for natural reasons, the quantity of wine made dramatically exceeds the permitted level, the character of the wine produced in such years tending to be light and fast-maturing. This 35 hectolitres per hectare is equivalent in normal bottle terms to 4,655 bottles per hectare, which clearly indicates the small production of estates or *domaines* only owning a few hectares each and is the reason why fine Burgundy is seldom abundant. Both growers and *négociants* count sales per bottle, not in cases of a dozen at a time.

The quantity of wine from the Pinot Noir grape will also be affected by the average age of the vines within the vineyard. Though it is quite normal to find vineyards where the vines are all the same age, this practice is poor husbandry. When replanting eventually takes place, the juice of the young grapes cannot be used for wines which are to receive the *Appellation* of their area (see page 133) until after the third year of the vine's life; the most satisfactory practice overall, therefore, is to keep planting on a regular and continuous basis so as to maintain the essential balance of the yield of the vineyard. In the past the replanting would take place vine by vine, but obviously this is a hangover from an era when labour was not difficult to obtain and when people had large families who could go out and work the patches of the vineyard. Nor, indeed, would it be possible to mix up very young individual vines with the matured stock – the *Appellation* would be difficult if not impossible to grant if this were done; replanting, therefore, takes place in rows or strips.

Vines can live as long as forty years, and even, exceptionally, reach sixty or seventy years in Burgundy. The oldest must be in Vosne Romanée – one hectare is planted with vines that are over ninety years old. When you look at such a vineyard, note how the older vines are thicker in their trunks and considerably gnarled at the base; as they age they produce fewer grapes but make fine wine. Remember too that after vines have been uprooted, the vineyard should be allowed at least one year to lie fallow – these fallow areas can be easily seen on the slopes by the tell-tale strips of bare land or, when this is sown with some restorative or tonic crop, by the fact that the crops on such fallow patches are close to the soil.

The juice of the Pinot Noir is without colour. This black grape variety is used in the production of Champagne. If you dare to pinch a ripening Pinot Noir grape, do not expect a mouthful of sweetness – the bitterness will dry your tongue. Indeed, very few grapes used for making fine wines are pleasant to eat.

CHARDONNAY

This is the noble white grape of all white Burgundy. The Chardonnay is responsible for the finest dry white wines in the world, ranging in style from the rounded character of Meursault, the lighter, more aggressive Pouilly Fuissé, the chalky dryness of Chablis and back again to the unique maturity of smells and flavours of the sublime Montrachets. The Chardonnay is grown all over the world and the wines it makes often win the sort of wine competitions that make national news and headlines in the international trade press.

The possibility of greatness being so close, it is not surprising that the Chardonnay is demanding in the way it is cultivated. The same quantities per hectare are allowed as for the Pinot Noir but, in the initial stages of wine making, the fermentation of Chardonnay wines takes longer than for wines made from the black grapes.

In the vineyards of villages where both red and white wines are produced (such as Chassagne Montrachet), it would be impossible for the beginner to select and know for certain whether a plant is Chardonnay or Pinot Noir, until the period from when ripening has begun to colour the grapes in July up until the vintage. So do not be put off if the difference is not apparent. When the colour of the two varieties does reveal itself, during the high summer, ownership of the land may be so diffuse that black and white grapes are planted side by side and then you can tell. The vines are planted 1 metre (1 yard) apart and grow 1 metre high.

I cannot resist a comment on some of the Chardonnay wines that I have tasted from other vineyards. The policy of many of the producers outside Burgundy is to label the wines according to their grape variety only ('varietal' is the U.S. term, 'cultivar' the South African). I believe these terms are misleading and confusing, though obviously the intention of those who label their wines in this way is the exact opposite. Yet is it helpful to the consumer, who wants to drink good wine, to have growers claiming that their use of the two noble grape varieties of Burgundy will – or even can – result in wines that can contribute exactly the same sort of pleasure and satisfaction to the drinker? Grapes are too strongly influenced by soil, weather and vinification, in my opinion, for a wine to be marketed only under grape varieties named on the label – especially if the wine concerned does not need, by local regulations, to be 100 per cent made from those particular grape varieties. Should not the name of the area or the shipper mean more to drinkers of fine wines than the grape variety? Unless discrimination is exercised and some knowledge of the subject is gained, the international wine drinker risks believing that a Chardonnay from the Nappa Valley will taste the same as a Chardonnay from the Mâconnais!

GAMAY

Mention must be made of the Gamay grape as it is still grown in very limited quantities in the Côte d'Or, especially in the Hautes Côte de Beaune and in the Hautes Côte de Nuits. Blended with the Pinot Noir, on a basis of two-thirds Gamay and one-third Pinot Noir according to the regulations, it produces Bourgogne Passe Tout Grains. This *Appellation* is rarely seen outside Burgundy, although certain shrewd shippers manage to obtain a little from time to time for export markets – it is therefore a rather curious wine, well worth sampling when you get the opportunity.

Gamay wine can never be included, except in Passe Tout Grains, in any wine coming from the Burgundy region that wishes to bear any of the A.O.C.s reserved for Burgundy. Further to the south the Gamay produces Beaujolais and the Mâconnais wines of fruity freshness. There is a village of Gamay, adjacent to Chassagne Montrachet, on the main road RN6, but there is little evidence to suppose that the Gamay grape took its name from the village or vice versa.

ALIGOTÉ

This white grape, used wholly for white wines, is slightly sharp and dry in taste. The vine is grown in varying quantities throughout the Burgundy region and the wine is sold at a modest price; it is always put on the market while young, for the hallmark of Aligoté is its freshness and cleansing acidity. Being a cheap wine from a famous area there is a real threat to its future production, for Aligoté vineyards are now being replanted with Chardonnay which, according to the position of the vineyards, may entitle the wines made to a higher and therefore more pricey *Appellation*, and thus get the grower a higher price too. Although Bourgogne Aligoté is sold only under this generic title, if you see a grower's bottling using the Aligoté grape, it will probably indicate, by the name of the grower's village, which particular area is responsible for the wine. Favoured sites for Aligoté in the Côte d'Or are the higher slopes, for the vine is hardy and it is also particularly worth mentioning the villages of Pernand Vergelesses, next to Corton, Savigny-lès-Beaune and, in the Côte Chalonnaise, Bouzeron in the region of Mercurey.

There is an excellent way of seeing good Aligoté at the Caveau de Dégustation at Marey-lès-Fussey.

Continue through Pernand Vergelesses into the wild country

behind the Bois de Corton, following the signs to Nuits St. Georges. Up on this plateau vineyards are well above the normal altitude recommended for the vines' comfort but today's improved technology has given the growers fresh heart and their efforts have had splendid results, especially for the Aligoté. A Burgundian lunch can also be taken at the Caveau de Dégustation. It is the Aligoté wine which, blended with cassis liqueur, makes the Burgundian apéritif *vin blanc cassis*, or *Kir* (see page 47). This is a good drink for conquering tiredness and refreshing any palate jaded by too much Burgundian food and wine.

Bourgogne Aligoté has never been easy to sell in the U.K. One suspects that, in the bad old days, it was occasionally used as a blending wine for bulk shipments that ought to have been entirely Chardonnay. An interesting tasting would be to observe the difference in style and character of different Aligoté wines by comparing those that come from the Chablis region (quite chalky), the Côte d'Or (firmer and fatter) and the Côte Chalonnaise (possessing higher acidity and generally greener). Personally I favour the Aligoté of Chablis for straight drinking, and the Chalonnaise Aligoté for the blend in *vin blanc cassis*.

The Vineyard Cycle

Some knowledge of what is involved with the cultivation of the vine, month by month, throughout the year can help the reader to gain a general idea of the annual cycle of events that produce Burgundy. It isn't just picking grapes in the autumn! At weekends and even late into the evening those who own small plots will go to work outside the hours of their own regular jobs. If you see people in the vineyards, here is what they may be doing in different months, whether they are self-employed or working for an owner. Some of the tasks on which they are engaged may be routine; others require skill and experience. Women and even quite small children will take part and, even though the work is hard, it is a dedicated routine, often carried on in extremes of wet and cold as well as in the heat of summer. It is back-breaking, too, because the vines are pruned low, so that anyone expecting to earn easy money for holiday picking is destined to find out the hard way: by spending hours doubled up so as to get at the grapes.

The curious double-bellied baskets, used only in Burgundy for gathering grapes, are extremely heavy to carry when full so, to lighten the load, plastic hods have today been introduced. They also possess the advantage of being easier to keep scrupulously clean – wickerwork can harbour infection, picturesque though it looks.

VINEYARD CALENDAR

January. The vines are pruned. Skill is needed in judging where the pruning should be done, so that the branches of the plant may be trained along the wires that support them during the exuberant period of flowering and then while the grapes are developing. If the branches are too short, the grapes will not be abundant. If they are too long, they may sag to the ground, risking the embryo grapes becoming chilled in the spring frosts or, later, getting rotten by being in contact with the earth. The system of pruning in the Côte d'Or is known as the *taille Guyot* (see page 34). It enables the vines to enjoy maximum exposure to the sun and air, without risking getting battered by rain or, worse, hail, and being too heated by the sun later in the year.

February. Pruning goes on and should be finished in this month. The weather often hampers work outside, but this is a time when equipment of various types is prepared.

March. The soil that was placed protectively around the vines to shield them from frost and possible snow in the winter is now raked away, so that they are able to receive the benefit of the sun and air. A special type of tractor is used to aerate the earth in the vineyard or, if the plot is small, this is done by hand. When a vineyard has been replanted, this is the time when the young vines are grafted on to disease-resistant root stock.

April. The vineyard is generally tidied up now that spring is coming. The prunings and trimmings of the vines are burned and the wires along which the tendrils of the vine will be supported are fixed. The young vines are planted.

May. There is still a danger of frost. The 'Ice Saints' (SS. Pancratius, Servatius, Boniface and Sophid) whose festivals are celebrated in mid-May represent a critical period, hence their name. A frost now can prevent the flower of the vine forming, so small heating pots and other warming devices appear in vineyards as safeguards. At the same time, weeds are removed – either by ploughing or else by hand – since they would take the nourishment from the vines. The vines are also probably sprayed against various diseases, especially mildew, with copper sulphate solution that turns their leaves bluish in colour. Nowadays many highly mechanised devices do this spraying, but you may also see men with sprays carried on their backs, directing the nozzle of the spray with their hands.

June. In this month the vine should flower – tiny flowers that nevertheless give a pungent scent to the vineyard when they open. Ideally, the flowering should take place within a short time and not be interfered with by rain or cold weather. The best shoots of the vine are now attached to the wires and any that are superfluous are cut away. Spraying probably goes on.

July. The vineyard may be ploughed again – it is getting warm and the aeration is necessary. Weeds must also continue to be removed, unwanted shoots cut off and spraying continued.

August. Many people in France are on holiday during this month, but the wine maker will be getting his cellar ready for the vintage. Vats and casks must be cleaned and prepared and machinery checked and put in order. Weeding must go on in the vineyard. By now, the black grapes will have begun to turn from yellowish-green to an increasingly dark purple.

September. The white grapes swell and become an almost luminous greenish-yellow. The black grapes fill out. This is vintage month and picking usually starts in about the third week. If weather permits, the grapes are gathered as they are judged to be ripe but not overripe, and are taken to the cellar to be crushed and the juice allowed to begin the process of fermentation. Pickers who are self-employed usually work all the hours of daylight, in a favourable season, while they have need to do so; other bands of pickers work to a more regular routine, but a vintage day is invariably long.

October. The vintage goes on into at least the first and second weeks. After it has finished, the vineyard is fertilised and any new plantations that may previously have been lying fallow are now prepared for planting by deep ploughing. In the cellars, the process of finishing and appraising the new wine goes on.

November. Soil is raked over the vine roots to protect them during the winter. Non-productive shoots and dead twigs are pruned for kindling wood. Sometimes the shoots and twigs will be burnt in the vineyard, showing spirals of light grey smoke against the wintry background.

December. The November tasks are continued in the vineyard and in the cellars the wine-making equipment is cleaned and put away, while the new wine continues to 'make itself'.

We can start the story of how Burgundy wines are made in February, when vineyard work begins again. The winter months are spent by the growers working in the cellar, watching over the new wine from the previous vintage and preparing the older wines for bottling in the spring.

There are no precise bottling dates, as these decisions are entirely left to the grower or shipper, but for red wines it would be quite normal for a grower to have three vintages in his cellar in February – the new wine, and the wines of the previous two vintages. However, earlier bottling of Burgundy has found some new advocates today, and maturation in wood has been shortened by many growers, so as to release their wine for sale at an earlier date. Every month that a wine, either in wood or in

Filling the vat (cuve) with grapes during the harvest

bottle, occupies space in a cellar costs money for its keep. This is often forgotten by the drinker. It should be remembered that the local wine market in Burgundy or, for that matter, in the other wine regions of France, is accustomed to drinking relatively fine wines much younger than the customers of the export trade.

During February and March there will be plenty of cellar activity in preparing export orders ready for despatch after the worst winter cold is over. No fine wines should be shipped in the extreme cold or even the heat of the high summer. They may suffer seriously if they travel then. While writing this chapter, I heard of a container of a thousand cases of excellent Burgundy being offloaded on to the dockside of New York and simply left outside over a weekend. It was a disaster – all the white wines threw a crystal sediment as a result of being chilled so brutally. This does not necessarily affect the flavour at all, but the U.S. market hates deposits or sediment in bottles, suspecting their presence as somehow indicative of a faulty wine (an error, but the U.S. buyer wants only 'star-bright' wines).

PRUNING

In the vineyard in late January or early February, the grower must organise the first pruning of the vines, and this involves care and detailed attention. The purpose of pruning is to control the future growth of the vine and eliminate unwanted shoots. In this work, the laws of A.O.C. governing the method of pruning must be observed. For the Côte d'Or the *taille Guyot* is the adopted pruning style. It can be described briefly: the main branch of the vine (*la baguette*) is trained along a wire some 30 cm (11¾ in) from the ground. Above that is a double wire, to which the shoots of the main branch are tied and, to complete the trellis effect, a further single wire runs along the top. These wires are held taut by embedded wooden posts.

Each year the vine is pruned to retain two branches, the *baguette* as mentioned, and another, the *caisson*, which is the replacement branch for the following year. Just occasionally you will see an experimental pruning method – *taille haute* – where the vines are trained higher off the ground, according to the theory that they thus more easily escape late spring ground frosts and excessive summer heat. In Alsace and Germany this method has been successful, but so far it is too new in Burgundy to know whether permission will be granted or even recommended for its use with the better quality wines.

During the spring, when the chance of frost has virtually disappeared, the earth-covered vine roots are cleared to allow the young shoots to receive a circulation of fresh air. Then they will sprout healthily in April.

There has been an experiment at the Domaine St. Michel in Santenay, where plastic sheeting was used to cover the roots of young vines. Apparently great success in protection has been gained, although the wind causes a flapping of the sheets and a hideous high-pitched whistle hits the ears.

POTENTIAL HAZARDS

Before taking the wine making procedure further, a look at some of the potential hazards to which the vine is exposed will help to illustrate the constant battle the vineyard proprietor wages.

Frost.   If spring temperatures fall below freezing (as low as – 4°C or 25°F, the vine is likely to suffer a diminution of eventual yield. If a grower thinks late spring frosts are likely, he will delay pruning and will wait until 15 May, the period of the 'Ice Saints'. Once it is safely over, vintage prospects are hopeful.

Hail.   This can cause local but cruel damage. In some regions noted for their exposure, the risk is sufficiently great for experiments in cloud dispersal by aeroplane to have been tried – though no one reports much success to date. Hail, battering the stems of the vine and leaving permanent traces, weakens it and destroys the vegetation. I have seen a vineyard at Chassagne Montrachet lose 30 per cent of its possible quantity in one day in June 1974. If the grapes are already formed, hail can split and destroy them. The flavour of an otherwise successful wine can also be subtly and adversely affected by hail.

Coulure.   This is when the partly formed grapes drop, rotting, from the vine. *Coulure* is transmitted by virus disease or infected grafting. It usually results from wet and cold weather at the vine's flowering time in June, with subsequent destruction of flowers and small berries. The white grape, Chardonnay, is more susceptible than the red Pinot Noir to *coulure*, although the treatment is the same. One must remove the infected vine, disinfect the soil and replant a young, healthy vine.

Millerandage.   A result of slight *coulure*, when bunches of grapes do not fully ripen, *millerandage* leaves only small green berries on the vine. If these bunches reach the wine making stage, they impart a harsh and bitter flavour to the wine.

Oïdium.   Also known as 'downy mildew', oïdium is a fungus disease appearing during warm, humid weather. The vine leaves and grapes will be spoilt by black stains and small, unpleasant moulds during June and July. Preventive vine-spraying with sulphur is therefore essential during early summer before the flowering, and again before the *véraison* (the time when the black grapes start to turn red from their original white colour). If oïdium is detected early, it may not be necessary to dig up the vine as there are now strong disinfectant sprays available to deal with it.

Mildew.   This is another fungus disease which occurs during humid weather. If it is allowed to develop, the leaves will fall, the berries lose their food lifeline and, should any infected grapes be harvested together with healthy grapes, the resulting wine will have an acrid taste and lack colour. The treatment of mildew involves spraying with Bordeaux mixture, which is a copper sulphate and dissolved lime solution. Helicopters have been introduced for spraying at speed and they are amazingly accurate, aided by the coloured discs seen standing in the vineyards as markers of the vine rows. (Owners pay heavily enough for spraying to be unwilling for neighbours to benefit as well.)

SUMMER IN THE VINEYARD

The vineyard calendar takes a major step forward in early June, when the grower will anxiously await a healthy *fleuraison* – the flowering of the vine. These flowers are not spectacular – indeed, they have to be looked for by the untrained eye and seem merely tiny flowers on the vine shoot. But they are most attractive in their smell, being fragrant and slightly musky. On a still day, in the early evening, a walk through the vines, particularly uphill, can be a conscious stroll through scent. The delicate fragrance is elusive but, once experienced, never forgotten.

During this time, spraying by hand, tractor or helicopter is a major activity and the growers watch carefully for signs of vine disease, and observe the progress of each plot.

By July and August, the vines should be growing rapidly, following the training on wires established during the pruning. If the growth at vinetop level becomes too abundant, there is a lopping to clear the way through to the grapes for the sun's rays and to concentrate the feeding process into the grapes, not into unwanted leaves.

As the vintage takes place traditionally a hundred days after the flowering, this high summer period can be seen as vital with regard to balanced weather conditions. Hours of sunshine, some gentle rain, low humidity, no hail and no storms – that is the ideal. These climatic conditions cannot be helped by man, as the laws of A.O.C. do not permit irrigation, even in hot summers lacking rain. Thus nature takes the major part in deciding the quality of a vintage. Fortunately, in Burgundy, it rarely lets the grower down; with improved viticultural knowledge, the number of years hitting low points have become fewer. To date, 1968 was the last real disaster.

When September arrives, the vintage is only a few weeks away, by which time all the preparations to receive the harvest must be completed. The fermentation oak vats are thoroughly cleaned and scrubbed; the *paniers* (grape pickers' baskets) are brought out and repaired; the grape presses are checked for working order. Cellars are cleaned and tidied and those on holiday return for the high spot of the vineyard year.

VINTAGE TIME

The next decision the grower will face is the date of picking the grapes (the *vendange* or vintage). Science can assist him by providing an analysis of the juice of sample grape bunches, which can now be taken from day to day or even hour to hour, but the weather remains the greatest factor in determining the quality of the crop.

In recent Burgundy vintages, there have been several fine summers with an inevitable anticipation of great vintages, which have been spoilt or altered by heavy rain coming at vintage time. Rain will increase the quantity of wine by swelling the grapes, but the loss of quality will be noticeable by the lack of body in the wine. Will the grower start when the grapes are ready early? Or will he wait, in the hope of continued sunshine to improve the grapes further – and risk rain spoiling

Traditional hand press

the crop? Whatever the decision, vintaging usually starts between 20 September and 19 October.

In the Burgundy region, vineyard holdings are small and friends and families join together for the picking, leaving little need for much outside labour to be imported for the tiring, back-breaking work so close to the ground. Everyone who can picks, the oddly shaped double baskets peculiar to the region then receiving the contents of individual *paniers* or trugs.

The *paniers Beaunois*, suspended on poles, are very heavy when full. The stronger *vendageurs* (pickers) get the job of lifting the full *panier* on to the transport for delivery to the presshouse.

At this point the A.O.C. laws demand a certificate for each travelling load of grapes, thereby beginning the control and record of quantity of the wine. The majority of growers in the Côte d'Or vinify their grapes themselves (other wine regions noted for quantity and less historical fame use a co-operative system extensively and successfully for vinification). In very abundant years, some grapes are sold to the *négociants* so that the shippers make the wine. But the sale of grapes in Burgundy by the grower to the shipper is a declining practice today.

When the grapes arrive at the presshouse, they will be analysed again for sugar and acidity content, giving the information necessary for judging if *chaptalisation* is needed. Knowledge of the future alcoholic strength is important if the wine wants to claim an A.O.C.

CHAPTALISATION

Chaptalisation is a practice widely used in Burgundy to bolster wines which are likely to have insufficient natural sugar in the grape *moût* (must) – the juice before it becomes wine – to make an acceptable wine, with no trouble involved during the fermentation. The process is named after Napoleon's first Minister of Agriculture, who issued the first decree authorising the already-known process. The wine yeasts feed on the grape sugar and cannot work satisfactorily if there is not enough. Growers are therefore permitted to add up to a maximum of 200 kilograms (440 lb) of sugar per hectare (2.4 acres) of vines during fermentation; they must not, by this method, increase the eventual alcoholic strength of the wine by more than 2°. This long-established addition of sugar must not be overdone; its object is to balance any complex constituents of the wine more successfully than has been done by nature.

Chaptalisation should not be considered a practice to be criticised adversely if it is handled responsibly, because the weather conditions of the Burgundy region rarely allow for sufficient ripening to fulfil the wine's natural sugar requirements and to convert the must into wines of body and substance without the addition of sugar during the first stage of fermentation. Only if *chaptalisation* is exercised to excess will it impair the delicate fragrance and harmonious flavours normal in the Pinot Noir grape exclusive to fine Burgundy. By contrast, Burgundy wines made without *chaptalisation* would, in most years, be disagreeable – thin and poor travellers, because of their lack of alcohol. (In countries of the world where Burgundy grapes are used to make wine without involving the process of *chaptalisation*, it can be interesting to note the slight but definite difference that is made by the omission of this process – yet another reason why I do not like wines to attempt to imitate Burgundy in any way.)

PRESSING

Ideally, grapes will be pressed immediately they arrive at the *fouloir égrappoir* – a cylindrical press that crushes the grapes but not the pips and also strips the berries or individual grapes off the stalks. The old wooden press, turned by hand, is a romantic antique today. The juice and pulp from the crushing is then pumped to the oak fermentation vats. Some growers and more shippers have purchased enamel-lined vats which are easier to keep clean, for at this stage the young wine is susceptible to infection. It should be realised that these vats in which the fermentation takes place are not the vats or vessels in which the wine will subsequently mature. They are used purely for the fermentation stage.

The manner in which the grower carries on the vinification will determine the character and quality of the resulting wines. Obviously this is the point at which the differences in making red and white wines become apparent, but before indicating these differences, a short restatement of the 'what' and 'how' of fermentation may give some understanding of the art of the vintner.

FERMENTATION

Before the experiments of Louis Pasteur in the mid-1850s, the chemical process of fermentation was little understood. Pasteur's work defined the actual conversion of the natural sugar in the juice and must into carbon dioxide and alcohol. The agent for this conversion is the 'bloom' on the skin of the ripe grape, which contains the yeast/enzymes (*Saccharomyces cerevisiae*). Most of the chemical constituents present in the must remain after fermentation, though the sugars are greatly reduced and alcohol, with esters and some new acids, appears.

In practice, the juice and pulp will be pumped from the press into the traditional oak vats or, today, into tanks. These are not filled to the top as the fermentation process is violent enough to overflow the vat when in full action.

Red Wines

Once the fermentation vat is filled to the correct height, it will depend, usually, on the overall temperature as to whether the fermentation begins immediately. The natural range of temperatures for fermentation is between 22°C and 30°C (72°F and 86°F).

If the weather is cold and the fermentation is reluctant to start, then the cellars will be heated to get everything going, for the wine yeasts cannot work if too cold or too hot. Control of temperature during fermentation is vital and the growers will closely watch the temperature gauge on the vat. If it looks at all likely that the process is slowing down through cold, then they are prepared to help the process with the aid of pipes filled with hot water that pass round the cellar. Alternatively, if the must looks as if it is overheating, then cold water will be passed through these pipes or the cellar doors left open. It is during this part of the fermentation that analyses are taken to check future alcoholic strengths, in case some sugar needs to be added to the must.

Red Burgundy is a fully fermented wine with no residual sugar (grape sugar left in the finished wine). If you ever taste a Burgundy which has a definitely sweet flavour, then you may well be suspicious about its provenance. That extra, sometimes treacly sweetness should not be there.

While fermentation takes place, the gas given off by this process escapes and a pulpy mush floats to the top of the vat (this is called the *chapeau* or hat). This crust is often broken up and pushed down again to immerse all the skins, pips and their constituents of which it is composed in the fermenting juice. The fermentation will end once the sugar in the grapes is fully converted into alcohol. For red wines, six days on average will see the process complete.

MÉTHODE ANCIENNE

The expression *'méthode ancienne'* (old-style vinification) became fashionable a few years ago, and was used to describe a style of fermentation in which all the stalks were left in the must and the pulp was left in contact with the fermented juice for more than a fortnight. The purpose was to provide darker, fuller and more flavoured wines. However, *'méthode ancienne'* is a doubtful term because a study of Burgundian vinification reveals no definite historical references to this manner of wine making. Traditionally Burgundy wines were quickly fermented and the wine separated from the *marc* (pulp) after a few days.

Obviously, these fermentation decisions are entirely individual and the future wine must be judged on its merit. However, the slightly misleading term *'méthode ancienne'* is now less prominent in the commercial language of the Côte d'Or than it was a few years ago – I think for good reasons.

MATURATION

Once the grower decides his wine has had sufficient contact with the *marc* (pulp), the wine is pumped off into oak casks (*'une pièce'* is the Burgundy word for the local cask) to recover and begin the next stage of its life.

Transferring wine from large storage vats to casks for further maturation and development

Wine undergoes a secondary fermentation, the malo-lactic, in which the malic acid is converted into lactic acid. In red Burgundy, this will take about six months of slow, more gentle fermentation than the first stage and it is liable to stop and restart without warning. Some gas is then let off and, putting your ear to the *pièce*, you can hear a gentle bubbling. During this stage of its fermentation the wine will be unclear and most difficult to taste. Indeed, you should try not to do so. If you ever taste a red Burgundy which has a fine bead of bubble around the wine's rim, which then imparts a prickle on the tongue, you have probably got a wine that was bottled before the malo-lactic fermentation was fully finished. This fault still occurs rather too often in Burgundy, for the analysis can tell, with almost total accuracy, whether this secondary fermentation is finished or not.

During the early maturation of the wine in the wood, the grower will guard and nurture his wines with parental care. According to his judgement, several cellar tasks related to the new wine will be decided: the *collage* (fining) to clarify the wine; the *soutirage* (racking), moving the wine from one cask to another, leaving behind the cask deposit or *lie* (lees), and the *ouillage*, or topping up of the cask after the natural loss by evaporation.

The length of time the wine remains in cask before bottling will be decided by the grower or the *négociant*. If the grower sells

Tasting before racking (changing the wine from one cask to another)

his wine in wood, it can be removed to the *négociant*'s cellar for his staff to take over the care of it, though in some cases the wine may change ownership yet remain with the grower for later transfer, prior to bottling – it depends how individual business is done.

BOTTLING

Whoever takes the decision to bottle, this is a major event in the life-cycle of the wine. A fine and experienced palate alone will know when the correct time has arrived for the *mise en bouteilles* or bottling process.

Growers tend to have fairly simple bottling methods – well tried and traditional – although some cellars capable of making very fine wine create some anxiety for the health of their wine at bottling. Cleanliness and super hygiene are a necessity – look for it always if you visit the wine's birthplace. An old cellar may look picturesque, but, at bottling time, it ought to look surgically clean.

Négociants, by the style of their business, undertake regular bottling programmes with expensive fixed equipment. Progress

has been made in recent years in raising the standards of
filtration and sterile bottling has become the accepted practice.
When visiting cellars it is interesting to look out for the variety
of equipment now required to maintain a shipper's business.
Heavy sums in capital expenditure have been invested by
shippers, all of whom seek a high turnover of the cheaper wines
to justify the cost of such installations. To a certain extent, the
successful cheaper wines will help to finance the longer
maturation of the fine wines. It is the cheaper wines that are
required in quantity and it is by the quality of these cheap wines
that you should judge the standing and standards of a shipper.

White Wines

The fermentation of the white grapes usually includes all the
pulp, plus the stalks, which provide the essential acids for the
wine. In contrast to the red wines, the whites need a long initial
fermentation, this taking place in cask for the finer wines and in
vat for the lesser *Appellations*. It is possible for the secondary
malo-lactic fermentation to be carried on actually during the
first fermentation and whatever happens then, the cellars are
kept warm, so as to keep the wines in a constant state of
chemical movement.

Normally, white wines will be bottled earlier than the reds,
but this is an individual decision as to the style required and is
dictated by the experience and skill of the producer.

Vintages

On a journey through Burgundy old wines will be rare on
restaurant lists and in the retail shops. So do not imagine you
are visiting the region to enjoy vintages long since forgotten. As
in other areas of France, the wines offered will be recent
vintages, often regardless as to whether they have a reputation
or not. In fact, the 'off' years are taken up by the local
restaurant trade as they satisfy the local market.

Guides to vintages may be helpful but they must be treated
with due care and attention. Early – and often much publicised
– announcements about vintages are also dangerous, because
the art of Burgundy wines is best demonstrated in the blending
and careful *élévation* (in the sense of 'upbringing') of the wines
during their time in wood; many a vintage has eventually
surprised the consumer by its acceptability after bottling,
though an original forecast – sometimes it has to be said,
delivered by unqualified and inexperienced people – may have
been damning. Equally, some highly heralded vintages manage
to lose their reputation – an example is 1976 – because too
much is expected of them.

In a perfect world Burgundy vintages should really be written and talked about publicly only when the wines are bottled. Curiosity and possible commercial interest however, continue to praise or condemn before thoughtful tastings, undertaken at a later date, can appraise wines one to two years after their first fermentation. A lot can happen between vintage time and bottling. Without any resort to the much publicised illegal blending practices, the fine Burgundian wine grower or shipper can influence his wine almost beyond recognition, and the change from the wine as tasted while still in wood to the wine that comes out of the bottle can bewilder the inexperienced.

My advice is: do not be too vintage conscious. It is quite possible for interesting, even good wines to be made in what appears to be a disastrous vintage; this can happen because of micro-climatic conditions, the age of certain vines or other variable influences in viticulture. Actually, in poor summers, white wines are more likely to be successful than reds and this must be remembered so as to avoid prejudice and the possibility of missing an enjoyable drink.

RECENT VINTAGES

1969. A below-average crop succeeded in producing very high quality red wines. The lighter style of the Côte de Beaune reds are still drinking well (in early 1984); the finest of the Côte de Nuits can still be kept for a few years. Among white wines, however, the vintage is becoming old, except for the finest growths in Puligny.

1970. Very large quantities of wine were made in all areas and, while first appraisals reported pale wines, albeit with a fruity character, they were often thought to be short of stamina. Since then, however, the best wines have definitely prolonged their life. Given correct storage, the 1970 reds can still be enjoyed now, if you can find them. The white 1970s also suffered from a lack of body, but during their lifetime they had considerable acclaim. Now there is a tendency for them to maderise, so care should certainly be taken before ordering them.

1971. The only trouble with this vintage is the lack of it! Superbly rich, elegant red wines were made, balancing equal levels of acidity and fruit. The smaller wines have come round now, but those bearing any important *Appellation* can take a few more years to obtain the concentration of the bouquet and the finesse to linger on the palate which is the hallmark of a great wine.

1972. The large amount of acidity that caused concentration originally did eventually soften out by the late 1970s; only the finest red wines are now drinking well as the eventual balance of the wines is slipping. The white wines in the top A.O.C.s may survive but will be high in smell and quite heavy in flavour.

1973. A very large crop that caused vinification difficulties – extra *chaptalisation* was needed to build up a vintage lacking in strength. Few 1973s will have survived well to the time of writing (1984). The white wines were finer and those from the best vineyards may still be worth drinking.

1974. A vintage which at mid-summer looked exceptional, but was then spoilt by heavy rains at harvest time. By now (1984) most 1974s have probably exceeded their capability.

1975. Weather conditions were similar to 1974: a hot summer followed by heavy rain and hail caused rot, with a reduced crop. The red wines can now be forgotten. Some white wines were surprisingly good but may not last much longer.

1976. With the benefit of hindsight we can now see that the hopes of a great vintage in this year can no longer be maintained. There was quite a rush to lay down the red wines at an early date but strangely the vintage failed to develop, giving an impression of a reluctance to wake up. Whether we shall see a miraculous old age among the normally top wines can as yet only be a speculation. This possible disappointment should not be allowed to spoil the enjoyment of many 1976s that have fulfilled the best they can do – suffice to say that the greatness hoped for in the publicity surrounding the vintage has yet to become apparent. The white 1976s have been glorious, providing they were bought from the *négociants* or *domaines* specialising in the upbringing of great white wines. By now (1984) only the top A.O.C.s can be relied upon to have retained the balance of fruit and acidity needed to show older white wines at their elegant best.

1977. Owing to severe rot and uneven ripening caused by heat, then enormous rain and heat again late in the harvest, the quality of this vintage has been slated. Both in red and white wines, however, it has been possible to discover acceptable wines from those makers mentally equipped to cope with a different vinification. Amongst the reds, those of the Marquis d'Angerville in Volnay, Domaine Tollot Beaut in Chorey-lès-Beaune, and Corton, have risen above the normal levels of quality and surprised many tasters by their intensity of ripe flavour. For the white wines there was a distinct tendency to sharpness, though Prosper Maufoux, *négociant* in Santenay, and Domaine Gagnard Delagrange of Chassagne Montrachet showed outstanding wines.

1978. A relatively abundant crop, with the red wines displaying good levels of tannin, strong aromas and colours that have deepened with age. Maybe the vintage lacks the final concentration of power and delightful subtlety of the 'greats' but rarely will you be disappointed by 1978. The white 1978s were highly developed – they are best described as ample wines. While this is not necessarily a fault, the majority show some clumsiness which, in the best sites of Puligny, Meursault and the Corton Charlemagne vineyard, has begun to flatten out into lengthy, well-defined flavours.

1979. It took some time before the 1979s were given the kind remarks the vintage deserved. During the difficult period of world recession, no great attention was paid to a crop of just over average size at the time the wine was made. By 1981/82, with the wines then in bottle, the strength of the vintage became noticeable by its youthful toughness – a durability that will benefit many of the wines if they are kept another three or four years from 1984. Whether the vintage has enough fruit to preserve the present attractive composition will only be known when more maturation has taken place. For white wines 1979 has been generous, producing excellent wines – sturdy, with very agreeable flavours that can be drunk at their best now. Though fast disappearing from the market, the finest whites will keep, if stored sensibly, for several years before giving up.

1980. Another vintage of the Depression period – not that Burgundy prices ever really stopped increasing, despite the very limited public following in Europe at this time. First tastings of 1980s showed wines lacking in substance, too mild for consideration as *vins de garde* (laying-down wines). Now, as if to show how wrong first assessments can be, the 1980s have grown in stature to reveal some very 'juicy' wines, of lively fruitiness and delightful taste. They are not for long-term keeping, but through the decade many pleasant surprises will be unfolded. The quality of the white wines was a matter of discussion amongst the cognoscenti of Beaune, in that Louis Latour found no redeeming features in them while Robert Drouhin produced his usual thoughtful opinion that, subject to rigorous tastings, some decent white wines were to be found. Experience now shows that some 1980 white Burgundies were well made, but only in small quantities. Certainly 1980s should be drunk now so do not let them moulder away in a dark corner.

1981. The summer proved rather irregular as regards weather and the harvest did not excite local opinion, many wines showing initial astringency, paltry flavours and charmless character. Yet the challenge of Burgundy is well illustrated by the 1981 reds, because, now we can see this vintage in bottle, the *négociants* (more than the *domaines*) have made improvements in the quality by the quite legal blending of various wines within the same A.O.C. Perhaps 1981 red Burgundies will not provide exceptional bottles but, by following the reputation of certain houses, it is wise not to ignore the possibilities of uncovering a surprising richness in certain of the wines. The whites of 1981 are joyful, distinguished by some sensational bouquets and, with their hardish core, there is no harm in putting away some Puligny Montrachet, Meursault, Chassagne Montrachet and a Corton Charlemagne.

1982.   Rarely does one associate large harvests with top quality – save possibly the 1982 clarets! Though Burgundy produced some remarkable quantities in many areas, it has since been noted that those Burgundy vineyards yielding the most wine are now paying for it by a lack of colour, small flavours and a general weakness of body. Fortunately, the growers who disciplined themselves to a tight, severe pruning restricted their crop to the advantage of the final wine. Hence among 1982 reds a decent minority of wines can be expected to offer a lovely ripe fruitiness, and a soft, generous body that flatters the palate. They are not really for long keeping though should be all right until the end of the 1980s. The white wines may fall short in acidity, but world demand has hurriedly taken them for swift consumption. The top villages will be claiming a 'fine vintage' with every justification.

1983.   Shortly after the harvest, the miraculous warm weather of mid and late September then suddenly turned to intense heat, drying away the damp and limiting the rot that had set in. How the vintage will fare, time will tell.

Vintage charts, reports, guides or what have you, are always open to criticism, as undoubtedly my own will be.

Look out for the off-vintage, gradually learn to trust the shippers whose wines you enjoy by recording the taste impressions. It is no good blindly to follow one shipper or group of shippers because you are told X is 'a fine shipper'. Discover for yourself – do not accept reputations that can be commercially advanced without quality. Decide for yourself, remain open-minded, be critical and be reasonable enough to change your mind with grace. After all, remember – Burgundy is fun.

Other Burgundy Drinks

Cassis Liqueur.   A very dark, almost purple liqueur is made from blackcurrants – the French for blackcurrant is *'cassis'*. It is intensely sweet but more fruity in taste than syrupy. Cassis is used in a number of ways to flavour puddings and sorbets: marinaded blackcurrants are poured over ice cream, and cassis will enrich many of the confections so magnificently displayed in the shops. The best cassis is made in and around Dijon – Lejay Legoute and Védrenne are two of the best-known brands.

Kir or Vin Blanc Cassis.   Possibly the most famous use for cassis liqueur is to make the apéritif known as *'un Kir'* or *'vin blanc cassis'*. Traditionally, this is one-third cassis to which is added two-thirds of chilled Bourgogne Aligoté; it is served in a large glass, with no ice. The effect of pairing a sweet liqueur with a sharp, slightly acidic dry white wine is sensationally thirst-quenching.

The nickname *'un Kir'* comes from the late Canon Félix Kir, a tiny little man who was at one time Mayor of Dijon and a member of the Chamber of Deputies. He played a heroic part in the Resistance during World War II and out of affection and respect for him his favourite apéritif was renamed *'Kir'* – a delightful memorial to a great man.

Bourgogne Mousseux. To quality for the description *'Bourgogne mousseux'* or sparkling white Burgundy, the sparkling wine must contain at least 30 per cent of Bourgogne Blanc wine made from the Chardonnay grape. The main centres of production are Rully in the Côte Chalonnaise and Nuits St. Georges. Most *Bourgogne mousseux* will be qualified by the words *'Méthode Champenoise'*, this phrase indicating another *Appellation* requirement in that this *mousseux* will have been prepared by the same process as Champagne (secondary fermentation taking place in bottle). Plain *mousseux* wine can be sold when only nine months old, instead of two years as in Champagne and the methods and techniques involved are quite different.

The expression *'Blanc de blancs'* will sometimes be used on the label to show that the juice of white grapes only has been used to make the *cuve*. The phrase is not of much importance in this context. *Bourgogne mousseux* can also be used to create a sparkling *vin blanc cassis* and most restaurants and bars will serve this sparkling apéritif by the glass.

Sparkling Red Burgundy. The fashion for sparkling red Burgundy fell away sharply after World War II, partly perhaps because the world of which it was part also ceased to exist. Its reputation in the U.K. was made during Edwardian times and satisfied the late-night drinking of many habitués of the music hall. None the less, there has been a revival in the popularity of certain brands of sparkling red Burgundy in the U.S.A., Canada and countries of South America. There is still a substantial amount drunk, too, in the north of England.

Production follows the Champagne method and only wines entitled to the Bourgogne Rouge A.O.C. may be used. Geisweiler may be singled out as a leading shipper, also Chauvenet, both of them at Nuits St. Georges. Best described as a 'fun' drink, it can be quite useful for parties or buffets where a change from the normal helps the gaiety along.

Marc de Bourgogne. Here we have the local *digestif*, which is taken very seriously by the cognoscenti – most of them from outside the region, it has to be admitted. Marc de Bourgogne is the local brandy, distilled from all the mush that is left over after the final pressings – stalks, skins, grape pulp and bits in general. It is distilled by mobile stills, under strict government control and, by law, this has to be done in a public place. The result, when aged in oak casks, can be extremely fiery, and it is not the tipple for sensitive stomachs. But if you have a strong constitution, the aroma will fill your head and the subsequent unsubtle flavour will seem to set your soul alight – and a few other places besides. However, devotees insist on its presence after lunch and dinner, preferring the labels of Louis Latour, Bouchard Père et Fils, Belin, and Hospices de Beaune.

Fine Bourgogne.   This is the distillation of Burgundian wine, not the debris of the pressings, as with *marc*, and it is certainly a more refined spirit. Fine Bourgogne is a local curiosity of limited appeal but worth a try on the spot.

4

Bottles, Labels and Buying

Before attempting to understand the labels of Burgundy wines, it is necessary to recognise the shape of the principal bottle. The sloped neck of this type of bottle is not exclusive to Burgundy and, although the shape is generally referred to as the Burgundy bottle, it is in use for other wines, mainly those of the Loire and the Rhône. In some regions, however, although the shape may closely resemble the *bouteille de Bourgogne* it may not be identical in measurement and exact proportions.

In the vast wine areas of the South of France such as Hérault, Roussillon and Languedoc, there seems to be no established tradition regarding the shape of the bottles used, so that it is up to individual firms and the Burgundy shape may be used together with the Bordeaux bottle (with squared shoulders) and the 'Hollandaise' (a dumpy shape with a long neck).

The various sizes of bottles found regularly in Burgundy are:
Magnum. This holds two bottles and is usually 1.5 litres (2.5 pints) in capacity. The magnum size is much less common in Burgundy than in Bordeaux, though undoubtedly its use is on the increase, and people are buying more big bottles today.
Bottle. This holds 75cl., 73cl. or 70cl. All French-bottled wines must carry the contents of the particular size on the label, usually in the left or right bottom corner. Until recently Burgundy bottles were traditionally of the 75cl. size, holding ¾ litre (1.3 pints) and this is still true as regards many wines. Modern legislation, however, has become more precise in its requirements for measuring the contents of bottles. This has resulted in some bottles, which are marked 75cl. in the glass on the foot of the bottle being only 73cl. in their actual contents. In fact the 73cl. content is probably the most accurate because the cork takes up space and, with time, the wine may also become slightly ullaged. The ullage is the air space between the cork and the surface of the wine, which may increase due to slight evaporation.

A word of warning on bottle size: since the price increases at the 1976 vintage – which reflected sharply on the world market – several of the lower A.O.C.s of Burgundy were bottled in 70cl. sizes. There may well be a market for such a size, but look before you buy, because this bottle will hold less than the others.
Half bottle. This holds 37.5cl. In most cases it is an unsatisfactory size – too small for some, too much for others,

certainly not enough for two people. It can be of some use as an
apéritif size, to lead on to bigger things.

Échantillon. This is the name for a trade sample – a tiny
bottle.

Labels

First, it must be stated firmly that anyone with a spark of
interest in Burgundy wines needs to be able to achieve instant
recall of a number of things when viewing bottles in shops or,
even more quickly, when seeing a restaurant wine list. Try to
remember certain essentials when buying or ordering. A label
can never tell you exactly what the Burgundy tastes like.
Remember never to 'drink the label'. Just because the name
and vintage appear great, and you have heard them, do not
automatically assume that the taste of the wine will be equally
great. Go directly to the wine and let it speak for itself. Leave
your critical consciousness open and do not be over-impressed
by presentation. Certainly in Burgundy the best-dressed bottles
often contain the dreariest wines; conversely, the finest wines
may bear dingy and unimaginative labels.

Most Burgundy bottles have two labels, a neck label (*la
collarette*) and a body label (*l'étiquette*).

The neck label should really only specify the vintage and the
shipper's name (growers rarely put their name on it). Meaningless expressions meant as descriptions that are as yet
uncontrolled by regulations and which are intended to give the
wine commercial appeal may also appear, such as: 'Grand Vin
(de Bourgogne)', 'Grand Vin de Réserve', 'Vin Supérieur',
and so on.

The body label is important. From it the significant
information will be available. First, it bears the name of the
wine. You should note that any wine grown in Burgundy and
offered as Burgundy must be an *Appellation Contrôlée*, wine
coming from one of the Burgundy A.O.C.s (listed on pages
139–40). On this list there are generic wines (such as Bourgogne
Rouge or Blanc), these sometimes being qualified by a *marque
deposée* (trade mark) – for example, you may see an A.O.C.
Bourgogne Blanc, 'Comte de Chartogne', from the firm of
Jaboulet-Vercherre.

The wine may be a village wine from a legally delimited
(defined) area, such as Nuits St. Georges. It may be a village
wine, also bearing the specific vineyard from that village – for
example, Volnay Clos des Chênes. It may be a vineyard so
famous and historically fine that it has earned its own
Appellation, for example, Le Musigny from Chambolle
Musigny. Here the words 'Chambolle Musigny' are not
obligatory on the label. An extra example pertinent in this

context is **Bonnes Mares**, as this is a vineyard of its own that straddles two village *Appellation Contrôlées*, Morey St. Denis and Chambolle Musigny. Both can be used – but not both names together.

Many Burgundy firms sell wines where the label gives no specific A.O.C. This can be taken to imply that they are wines blended to resemble certain Burgundy styles, but which are far lower in price. They are marketed to satisfy some of the local demand and any export market hoping to supply carafe wines made in Burgundy style. Brand names proliferate in this category. The wines can be pleasant.

The Names on the Labels

SHIPPERS

The term 'shipper' obviously means the man or the firm who ships wine, either operating in and from the region of production (or several regions), or else based in an export market whence the buyer will travel to make purchases in the wine areas. Sometimes a shipper will specialise in, or at least concentrate on, the wines of one region or type; sometimes the firm of shippers will deal in a wide range. It may be loosely understood that the word 'shipper' signifies a wholesaler – but a shipper may also, in an export market, deal directly with the public, acting as a merchant, holding licences to handle wines in wholesale quantities and also by the single bottle. So a merchant may also be a shipper and a shipper a merchant. The *'négoce'* is a term used in French to signify the shippers as a group – these shippers may also include the owners of vineyards or estates.

In the U.K. the shipper's name may be that of a U.K.-based firm, such as H. Sichel & Sons (who do not own shops or sell directly to the public the wines they ship); or Corney & Barrow, (independent wine merchants, who also ship wines); or Grants of St. James's (who ship and, through their retail outlets, branches of Victoria Wine, sell direct to the public in their capacity as merchants) and my own firm, Laytons. We ship and we also sell direct to the public.

It is for firms to register their names in Beaune, Nuits St. Georges and other Burgundy centres in order to use the particular label specifying this when they export wines purchased in Burgundy; this label can carry weight in many export markets, because obviously a firm with standing in a region of production is assumed to have a special knowledge and experience of the wines. Some of us also make our own arrangements for cellarage in the region, which provides us with a valuable base. We retain immediate and direct control of the wines we buy. My firm, for example, use Marcel Amance et Cie, in Santenay, where we can bottle such wines as we wish. We are in close contact with our wines and they are not at risk from being moved, while still in wood, from where they have been made, selected and bought.

Up to now 'trust the shipper, my boy' has been a traditional piece of advice and it is possibly still true that it is a reasonable point of view. A bottle with a totally unknown shipper's name has started many an explosion in past investigations into wines of doubtful provenance and 'scandals' that have hit the headlines. Today, however, legislation requires that either an address or, in France, a code enabling wine to be traced to its source, should appear on the wine's label. So merely to 'trust the shipper' is a somewhat superficial counsel if Burgundy is to be appraised by high standards of critical appreciation.

The shipper from and buyer for an export market should not be content merely with receiving samples from sources of supply – however good – and placing his orders after tasting these on his own premises, as often happened in the old days. I think that a shipper should visit the Burgundy region several times each year if he is to work significantly with his suppliers, and this is what the respected buyers do today. Personalities, equipment, methods all change, and the buyer must be aware of possible competition and local market trends. Such bottles as he offers will be qualified by such phrases as *'Mise en bouteilles en Bourgogne'*, 'Bottled in France' and 'Bottled in the region of production'.

NÉGOCIANTS

The *négociant* is the French shipper. The town or village where he has his office and main cellars must be mentioned after his name. For example: Louis Latour (Beaune); Bouchard Père et Fils (Beaune); Faiveley (Nuits St. Georges); Henri de Villamont (Savigny-lès-Beaune); Prosper Maufoux (Santenay). These are only a few.

The firms of *négociants* remain the backbone of the Burgundy wine trade: their names need to be mastered before a full knowledge of Burgundy labels can be claimed. The styles of Burgundy they offer vary. So, often, do their prices, even for wines bearing the same name. Usually the corks are branded, mostly commonly by *'Mise en bouteilles dans la région de production'* (bottled in the region of production).

GROWERS

With the increase of bottling by the growers, more wines will be seen in the various chains of distribution – such as shippers and merchants in export markets – with their own label. To identify such a grower's label, look for an individual name or family as opposed to that of a firm. Quite often the label will also say *'Mise du propriété'*, or *'Mise en bouteilles par le propriétaire'*. All mean 'bottled by the proprietor (grower)'.

DOMAINES

In this context it is misleading to assume – as lovers of red Bordeaux may do – that *'domaine'* is exactly equivalent to *'estate'*. Of course the word signifies this but, in Burgundy a *domaine* can be defined as several vineyards, possibly in various villages, singly owned, but of course vinified separately so as to maintain a scrupulous division between the different A.O.C.s that may be involved. These wines are subsequently bottled by the *domaine* and sold under such a label. For example: Domaine Parent, *propriétaire à* Pommard (Côte d'Or). (Apart from Pommard, this *domaine* also owns vineyards in Beaune, Volnay, Monthélie and Corton.) *Domaine* labels will be qualified by the words *'Mise du domaine'*, meaning *'domaine* bottled'.

There are some points of difference to notice between a *domaine* and a grower. First, a *domaine* will own a larger area of vines than a grower; second, a *domaine* will be more likely to bottle its own wines than a grower; third, a *domaine* may be managed on behalf of shareholders, so that, although there will be one concern immediately involved with the management of the vines and making and bottling the wine, the interests of the owners may be diverse.

OTHER LABEL INFORMATION

The various sizes of lettering on labels are controlled by the French labelling laws, although these need not concern us. These do ensure, however, that no wine name that should be clearly shown is in any way obscured, confused or detracted from by the use of any other name or word on the label.

A warning: one of the first achievements for a novice buyer of Burgundy is to recognise a phoney label. There are, even now, a few U.K. shippers attempting to pass off bottles from the Burgundy region as 'French bottled' when, by a study of the label, it is clear that they are not. The misleading expressions are: *'Mise en bouteilles dans nos caves'* (it depends where the *'caves'* are, London or Beaune?) and *'Mise par l'acheteur'* (yes, but where did the *acheteur* (buyer) do the bottling?). This practice is not widespread but in every trade there are a few small firms prepared to chance their integrity for commercial gain. So check the essentials before you buy if you want 'the real thing'.

The complete information required by law concerning the wine should always be clearly stated on a Burgundy label. This information comprises:

The wine's name – generic, village and/or vineyard;
The responsible person – foreign shipper, *négociant*, grower or
  domaine;
The vintage – the year of production;
The size of the bottle – contents' measure.

Certain traditional label expressions were once used to indicate the quality of the wine as assessed by the grower or shipper. These are now largely of mere historic interest and in my opinion it is best to ignore such expressions as: *'Tête de Cuvée'*, *'Première Cuvée'*, and *'Vieille(s) Vigne(s)'*. If a reputable firm does use them there's no harm done, but if an unknown one makes lavish use of them, this can be somewhat suspicious.

Another qualifying expression, *'Premier Cru'*, must be treated with caution, as there have been attempts to make several classifications of Côte d'Or vineyards, in a similar way to the classification of most of the main regions of Bordeaux. One might have thought that the arguments and, indeed, furious disputes attendant on these updatings of the Bordeaux classifications might have deterred the Burgundians or, at least, those who write about their wines, from trying to do something similar. Still, there are people who like things neatly put into categories (although it should never be forgotten that the Bordeaux classification of 1855, the most famous, was not made according to quality, but referred to expected prices). There have been several attempts at sorting out the Côte d'Or vineyards in categories of quality both by some of those in the wine trade and by various writers. Obviously the experience and interests of many of those concerned have affected the proposals they have put forward. It does not seem likely that any rigid, official classification will be imposed on what is already a somewhat complex wine region. However, there are some terms in use that may affect the prospective buyer, so I shall mention them. Although the top vineyards appear in each of these classifications, there are some sites claiming *'Premier Cru'* status without complete authority to do so. Occasionally a village name will be followed by *'Premier Cru'* or *'1er Cru'* (the same thing) but no vineyard name. This means that two *Premier Cru* vineyard wines of the same village have been blended together, so the wine loses its claim to a vineyard name but retains its *Premier Cru* entitlement. As long as you appreciate what is involved you are unlikely to be confused.

Knowing how to interpret a Burgundy label is something that will repay you, whether in terms of the quality of wine you get, or the money – and disappointment – that you are saved. Nor is it really difficult – it probably seems more so when details have to be written down. Indeed, you should look very sharply at any

label that does confuse you. Sort out the information on the
label and interpret it according to the facts. Then you will know
something definite about what the bottle contains. But never
forget that no label can guarantee quality: this is the sole
responsibility of the person who grew and made the wine, the
firm who bought and shipped it, and, eventually, the merchant
who offers it. His name and his alone is your 'guarantee'.

What is on the Cork

Questions are often raised about the branding or marking of
corks. The following expressions are normally found on the
cork:

> *Mise dans nos caves* – can be misleading because the *'caves'* may
> be anywhere
> *Mise dans la région de production* – bottled in the area
> *Mise au domaine* – bottled at the *domaine*
> *Mise à la propriété* – bottled by the proprietor
> Name of shipper
> Name of the *domaine*
> Name of *Appellation* – this is rare
> Vintage – also rare

Examination of the cork of a wine can provide certain
information – even if only that such-and-such a firm uses
sound, quality corks for its wines, whereas another firm trying
to cut corners, uses less expensive ones. The wine lover
accustomed to, for example, the detail customary on the corks
of fine Bordeaux may query the casualness of Burgundy cork
markings. There is no really satisfactory reason why Burgundy
growers and shippers do not use fully branded corks, with the
vintage and A.O.C. – it is a good question to ask on a visit. But
the answer will probably be different wherever the question is
asked.

Buying Burgundy – on the spot and at home

When you are in the region of Burgundy itself, don't be so
carried away by your enjoyment of the wines that you're easily
persuaded to pay fancy prices for wines offered on the spot. If
you can pause to do some basic calculations, preferably with
one or two good British wine lists for immediate comparison,
you'll often find you should wait to do your buying until you get
home. This has the advantage that not only may you actually
save on the purchase price and the business of transporting the
wine, but also you will be able to follow up with a personal
query to the merchant should you think there is anything wrong
with the wines once you taste them away from the region.

There are several new retail wine shops in Beaune, stocking a wide range of wines from a good selection of firms appropriately chosen as likely to appeal to the wine lover seeking a souvenir. The best is Denis Perret, offering wines from five firms: Drouhin, Bouchard Père et Fils, Louis Latour, Louis Jadot and Chanson Père et Fils; also recommended is the Vinothèque, which is totally independent. If you visit a cellar or tourist tasting room, there will usually be some inducement for you to buy wine, generally in a pack of three or six bottles in a specially designed carton. Again, don't rush to buy: a little mental arithmetic will quickly tell you the value – or otherwise. Bottles in the lower price ranges for use on picnics or if you are self-catering are possible purchases.

To buy Burgundy in Britain, or in any export market, whether for drinking immediately or for laying down for long-term maturation, it is essential to discover a wine merchant who both knows the subject and who can sincerely enthuse about his stocks of this somewhat complex wine. It isn't all that difficult. You can't buy Burgundy just by picking the name of a bottle off a list – any list. There must be some personal contact between you and the supplier. Write to or telephone the merchant – ideally, get to know him by visiting him at his place of business. If he holds tastings of Burgundies, this is an even easier way of establishing a relationship. Don't be shy about wanting to find out about him and why he lists the Burgundies he does: ask him how many times he has been to Burgundy – and when he was last there. A man who merely did a session there as a trainee twenty years ago is hardly likely to be alert to today's possibilities and problems; someone who makes regular visits or who is in constant contact with one or more of the shippers will know about current trends and how wines of particular growers and *négociants* may suit his public. If you can get your merchant to talk to you, you can soon judge as to whether his command of the subject is deep and sincere or not. He will, for example, be able to assess your requirements even in relation to the wines of other firms on which you can report to him. Nor should you be shy about telling him the circumstances in which you are likely to drink Burgundy – at formal dinners, for general entertaining – and the sort of prices that are within your range. It's a challenge to him to be of help.

A word of warning to the wealthy, who may be tempted by offers of very old vintages of Burgundy. These wines can be wonderful buys (however much you may have to pay for them) if – and it is an important 'if' – they have been kept in the same cellar throughout their period of maturation. Be somewhat wary of wines that have an old vintage date on their label but have been recently shipped from Burgundy. It is highly probable that the natural deposit that forms, and should form, in the bottle of such fine wines, may have been extracted by a mechanical device and the bottle recorked prior to shipment. This is done with good intent. Many export markets – notably the U.S.A. (although not the U.K.) – suspect any kind of sediment in a bottle of wine and refuse wines with 'bits' in them, so the Burgundians endeavour to give them star-bright wines.

Frankly, I think that this practice of removing the deposit, on which the wine feeds throughout its life in bottle, simply extracts the guts of the wine, so that a beverage that is weak and thin in flavour replaces one that might have possessed grandeur if it had been left alone. So try, if you do buy such wines, to ascertain that this prior 'decanting' has not taken place. This is another reason for getting to know a wine merchant, who will have the detailed knowledge of where your wines have been and how they have been kept.

HOW I BUY BURGUNDY – AS A BURGUNDY SHIPPER

The British market faces special problems with Burgundy, and these are unlikely to be solved within a year or two. Competing as we do with other export markets that have strong traditions for buying and appreciating Burgundy, such as Belgium, The Netherlands, Switzerland and, now, the United States, the present weakness of the pound sterling puts Britain at a great disadvantage. It is no use listing wines that are simply too expensive for the public to begin to think about buying them!

Whether or not the U.K. can remain an important and respected market for the wines of Burgundy – as it has been in the past – must now depend on how individual British shippers are able to give up time far in excess of what may be economic for their firms or, indeed, convenient for them as human beings, so as to search out stocks of wines that their countrymen can both like and afford. They must, too, circumvent various old methods of buying that are simply too costly. For example, no British Burgundy shipper these days can rely on simply receiving samples and tasting these in the offices of his principal, or on depending on what his interpreter may tell him as regards prices and qualities of wines when he travels in the country. He must make his own assessment as to the calibre of the source of supply, and impress such sources with his own abilities in being able to promote and handle the wines they may be offering him: if he can't hold his own in a business discussion with a peasant proprietor or a broker, he risks paying a higher price than he can really afford, not because of any sharp practice but simply because he is at a disadvantage now as regards money and must therefore stress his assets of knowhow and prestige.

Personally, as a London-based shipper conducting my own Burgundy business, I enjoy the constant challenge to me, as an individual. I would not want to be just an agent for one single Burgundy house, as the restrictions on my activities would be too tight for me to operate in the way I think is most effective for my organisation – and my customers.

A digression on my buying philosophy may be relevant, if it helps the reader to understand how these precious wines reach the lists of my firm. First, it's essential and prudent to establish firm and happy business relationships, in which each party has respect for the other. Spread friendship far and wide, always.

For firms who have limited resources of capital, it is a requirement not to hold large stocks of wine these days, but to seek suppliers who themselves are able to bear the responsibility and financial burden of stock continuity or maturation: to ensure continuity, stocks have to be held – and capital tied up – for a considerable time. In this context, the *négociant* fills the role of the ideal supplier; usually, such a shipper can also offer a more commercial approach to business transactions, by more fully understanding the business problems that are certainly attached to the operations of the British wine trade today.

In the case of my own firm, our Burgundy trade has developed sufficiently for us to have our separate connection in Santenay (where many of our wines are bottled), with Pierre Maufoux in the firm of Marcel Amance. Yet we – my colleagues and I – still continue to visit many other *négociants*, in order to search out bargains, appraise different styles of wines, and gain knowledge of ranges from which we can select wines of greater variety for our customers.

For me, to visit the cellars of growers, together with my broker and/or *négociant*, so as to taste the wines and make a selection, is the main work with which I, as a shipper, am really concerned. Others have different ways of doing business, and whether the result is good or bad is their affair.

To decant or not?

Travellers to Burgundy are sometimes surprised that, on occasions when really fine wines are served, they are poured straight from the bottle. If you want your wine decanted, you may have to insist, for the wine waiter won't ask you if you want it done and he may point out that there isn't any deposit – so why are you worrying? Even when you've got your way, he may have to go and look for a decanter – or ask you if you mind the wine being simply decanted into a clean bottle, or even the original bottle, rinsed free of its deposit.

So, why don't the Burgundians decant their wines? The previous paragraph gives some clue. In a luxurious eating place, catering mainly for the sort of tourists who demand inter-national food and often welcome what is sometimes referred to as *'le grand chi-chi'* of service, decanting may be done (albeit sometimes in an uninformed way). But in general it won't be, simply because the average Burgundian may not have what we understand by 'decanters'. Historically, the products of the major glassworks were much sought after and, in the eighteenth and nineteenth centuries, various new products, including decanters, were made in huge quantities, although they were not usually cheap. It is also perhaps significant that, at the period when decanters adorned the tables of the well-to-do in Britain, it was claret, with its heavier deposit, that went into them.

The Burgundian wine producer is, for the most part, a real countryman – in other words, a farmer – and he lives simply, spending money on essentials – which certainly include food and drink – but avoiding extravagance. His home is usually above his cellar and, when he wants wine, he goes and fetches a bottle and, after drawing the cork, puts it on the table. There is no elaborate service by house servants and, in the majority of restaurants, the staff (who may often be the owner's family) will be friendly and simple, rather than professionally smooth. This does not, I must admit, include the students of the various catering schools, such as those of Tournus, for example, who serve at some of the banquets given at Les Trois Glorieuses, and who impress by their adept and wholly skilled presentation of dishes. But generally catering is informal, however *haute cuisine* the dishes may be.

Incidentally, one of the possible reasons for the use in Burgundy of the enormous glasses that may, filled, hold one or more whole bottles of wine is, I suggest, so that the wine in such a glass may receive the aeration that it might otherwise get by pouring it into a decanter. But this doesn't make me like giant glasses any better: the excessive airing that a wine receives when it is swung round in something the size (and shape) of a storm lantern can sometimes result in it throwing off all its bouquet before the drinker gets more than a vague whiff of it! These giant glasses, sometimes brought out with much fuss, for a special – and expensive – red Burgundy, are really gimmicks, developed by restaurants catering for the sort of clientele that knows very little about wine, but likes a show to be made. Ask for an ordinary glass if such vulgarities are put before you.

There are other possible reasons why the practice of decanting has never been much followed in Burgundy. I have found the deposit in Burgundies to be firm, rather than in fine particles so that, if one pours carefully from a gradually inclined bottle without tilting it up and down and stirring up the sediment, this deposit will remain only in the last of the wine. But the French don't seem to mind it being in their glasses either and, maybe on account of their habitual thrift or because they think Anglo-Saxons are absurdly fussy about preferring wine to be bright and clear in appearance they will, unless you seize the bottle in time, tip out every scrap from a bottle, deposit and all. With red Bordeaux, the fineness of some of the deposit can make a wine cloudy if it is not carefully decanted, but this has not been my experience with even oldish red Burgundies.

Older red and white Burgundies should usually improve with decanting but the best time to decant before drinking can only be judged on the individual qualities of each wine. Recently I have been fortunate to taste old vintages of Chambolle Musigny les Amoureuses of the 1920s that needed two or three hours to show at their best. But, unless you know the wine extraordinarily well, it would generally be safe to decant one hour before serving and allow the wine to develop in the glass after pouring. One of the delights of both mature red and white Burgundy can be the immense depth of flavour, and this can only be fully appreciated once the wine has had a chance to blossom out by contact with fresh air after years of imprisonment in the bottle.

On the other hand, it may be – and one can only go by personal experience – that some Burgundies do not benefit from being decanted. At home I was once serving a fine Burgundy in magnums, which I had decanted. The wine was so good that I had to go down to my cellar and get some more bottles up, which I was obliged to serve immediately after drawing the corks. My guests all found the wine poured straight from the bottles much better! But this is the sort of thing that shows how impossible it is to make definite and general statements about Burgundy: each set of circumstances can make one change one's mind and every fine wine can require different treatment. You must go on tasting and experimenting and bear in mind that it is impossible ever to be definite about the best way to serve this wine – only try to avoid risking the bottle's contents being spoiled by careless handling.

5

Burgundy Wine Journey

You really need a car to explore Burgundy because the vineyards are essentially part of the real countryside. So it is worthwhile hiring one, even for a day or two and even if you also need the services of a driver. Excursions through the vineyards can be undertaken by means of the tours organised by the Office du Tourisme and the Syndicat d'Initiative in Beaune, but of course on these you can't stop where you wish.

No one should expect to see everything, even if several days or weeks are available, and naturally much depends on whether you are going to include visiting the many historic and architectural treasures in which Burgundy is rich, as well as looking at vineyards. I would not, anyway, suggest a hurried tour: you need to survey the landscape, observe the way in which the colour of the vineyard soil changes in different regions, note the curves and hollows of the plots, and bear in mind all that this may imply in terms of the wine that is being produced there. Take time to stop the car, study the vineyards both close to and from a distance, even if you are doing this in winter when the vines themselves look bare and dead. Look at the way in which the vineyards make a pattern with the stone houses and farm buildings and register this when you stand beside some quite small area planted with vines that make world-famous bottles of wine, possibly beyond your pocket except for special occasions. If you are able to do this in the heart of Burgundy, you will never feel quite the same about the wines again.

In each of the following sections, I have described something of the wines and specific vineyards for the benefit of armchair travellers, but you must make your own choice of routes and follow your own inclinations as to places to stop. In Appendix 3 you will find listed various useful works of reference. The Michelin Green Guide *'Bourgogne'* will assist with many places of general interest, although it is only available in French. As regards visiting cellars, I have indicated those that can offer this facility, though it is a courtesy to notify them in advance, if you can state an approximate time. (Don't forget the midday shutdown.) Michelin maps 66 and 70 cover the area, although for the Chablis region you will need 61 and 65 as well. Don't try to manage with any small map of France – you need a detailed one to follow the little roads that take you through the vineyards. The following itineraries all start from Beaune.

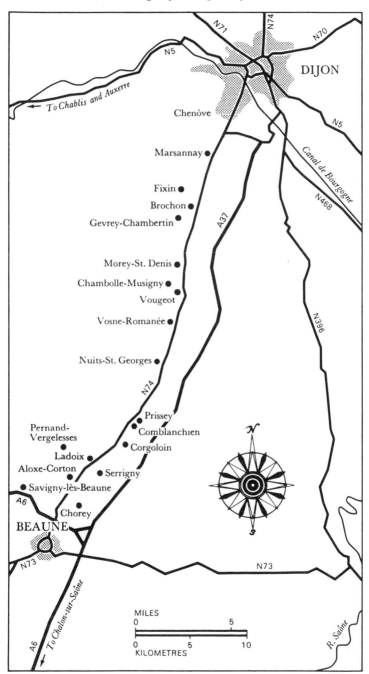

The Burgundy Region – Dijon/Beaune

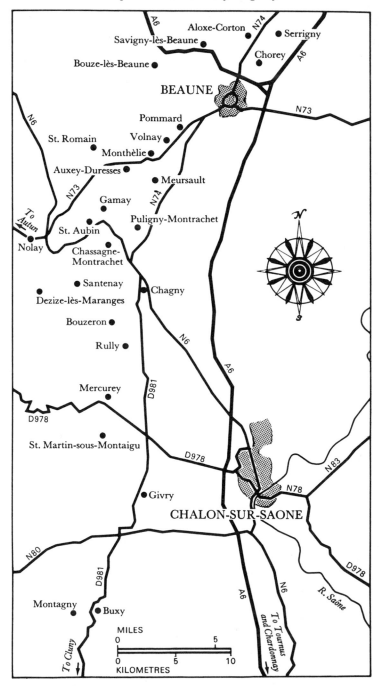

The Burgundy Region – Beaune/Chalon-sur-Saône

Possible Itineraries

If you have a whole day, this first itinerary will show you the entire Côte de Beaune. To follow it, leave Beaune on the N6 and, after about 1.6 km (1 mile), turn off to the right on the N73. After the branch-off, you will be able to see Pommard, Volnay, Monthélie, Auxey Duresses, Meursault, Puligny, Chassagne and Santenay (pages 97–109).

You should spare another whole day to see the Côte de Nuits. (You could do this in half a day by making an early morning start and by not stopping along the route, although to rush through in this way would obviously be a pity.) Leave Beaune by the Porte St. Nicolas going north, as if you were taking the old N6 to Dijon. At the first set of traffic lights the road to the left will lead over the Hautes Côtes de Nuits, through the top of the Bois de Corton, and come down at Nuits St. Georges. From Nuits St. Georges you can join the N6 again, going north and seeing Vosne, then leave this route at Vougeot and follow the vineyard road so as to see Chambolle, Morey, Gevrey, Fixin and Marsannay. After this you can return to Beaune on the new fast motorway (pages 74–87).

Another whole day is necessary to see Chablis. For this, take the motorway towards Paris and, after about a two-hour drive, leave it at the intersection marked Auxerre Sud and follow the signposts for Chablis (pages 67–74).

If you have only a half day available and want to see something of the town of Beaune itself as well as the Côte de Beaune, follow the same route as for the first day's itinerary, but, after Puligny, take the main road (N6) back to Beaune. If you are making the whole circuit (during which you will probably break for lunch in either Auxey or Meursault), you can also return to Beaune by the N6 (page 102).

For anyone really short of time, the Beaune vineyard will at least provide some idea of Burgundy. Take the road out of town in the direction of the Montagne de Beaune and Bouze-lès-Beaune. From this site you can enjoy a panorama of the vineyards. It can easily be done in an hour by car and in fact it is a very pleasant excursion on foot; you can either take the car part of the way or actually walk from Beaune. Try also to see something of Beaune itself (page 91).

If you have already explored part of Burgundy, perhaps the Côte de Nuits, then Aloxe Corton and the northern end of the Côte de Beaune provide an interesting itinerary, because the wines are now becoming widely known. The trip can be comfortably managed within a couple of hours, allowing the traveller to pay homage to the Corton Charlemagne vineyard *en route*. Leave Beaune by the Porte St. Nicolas, follow the RN74 to Aloxe Corton and then take the itinerary suggested on pages 87–91.

Another excursion can take half a day or be extended for a whole one if you lunch *en route* and then spend an afternoon seeing some of the art treasures and monuments, such as Cluny and Tournus, and the countryside in general. For this leave Beaune on the N6, going south. At Chagny take the N481 in the centre of the town down to Buxy, returning via Montagny, Mercurey and Rully. This part of the journey will take only about half a day unless you make several stops (page 109).

Anyone visiting Dijon must see the Ancient Palais des Ducs de Bourgogne, which is now the Musée des Beaux Arts. The Musée Perrin de Puycousin has an exhibition of objects relating to local life in Dijon and Tournus, and the Cellier de Clairvaux, built in the thirteenth century, is a regional tasting room.

Try to allow a whole day or at least a generous half to see Beaune, an attractive little town, where you can walk right round inside the old walls. Things of particular interest are, of course, the Hospices de Beaune, which is also known as l'Hôtel-Dieu and Musée; if you simply enquire for the 'Hospices' you may not be directed helpfully (page 93).

The Musée du Vin de Bourgogne is in the former Hôtel des Ducs de Bourgogne and shows every aspect of wine production, together with an interesting collection of *tastevins*, also the famous tapestry by Lurçat, showing wine, the source of life, triumphing over death. Among the many other works of art and things of historic interest, the tapestries in the Église Nôtre Dame should not be missed. In the narrow streets, picturesque and apparently unchanged, which lead off from the Place Carnot and Hôtel de Ville, you can wander about for hours. It goes without saying that the various shops, especially those selling food, around the Place Carnot and the Place du Marché, are usually irresistible for the gastronomic traveller.

The visitor to Burgundy will often remark on the serenity and calm of the villages, which only really seem to come to life during vintage time. How these villages mostly appear so deserted is a piece of French magic. The Frenchman lives behind his house – in every sense of the word. You will notice that there are no front gardens. The house-owner, when he is not actually away working, possibly in some vineyard quite distant from his home, may be in his cellar or out of sight elsewhere in whatever building he has by way of a workshop, or in the dumpy farm buildings usually shielded by an ancient but definitely forbidding high door or gate.

Chablis

For the traveller going south by car, Chablis is the first region of Burgundy. The Autoroute du Sud (A6) passes the area, with a conveniently signposted exit after two hours' driving from Paris. Today Chablis is of much less importance than it was during the Middle Ages, when this whole area, lower Burgundy, extended to the then large viticultural districts around the towns of Avallon, Joigny, Tonnerre and Irancy.

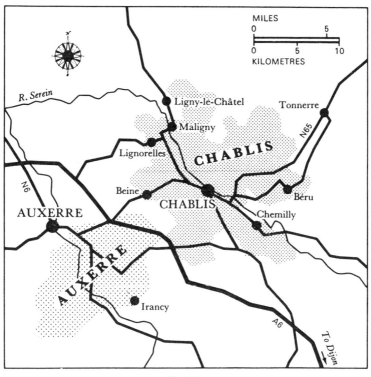

Chablis

The wines these districts make today are rarely seen outside the immediate vicinity. 'Chablis', as a generic title, gives its name to the wines from the many villages and hamlets surrounding the town, the starting point for all visits.

THE TOWN

First-time visitors will be surprised to find Chablis a small town for such a famous one – yet it is much the better for that, and is virtually unspoiled by twentieth-century developments. The town was owned by the French crown until the ninth century when it was given to the Church of St. Martin at Tours in the Loire. It remained in religious possession until 1789, when the French Revolution broke up the freehold ownerships.

Walk about in Chablis, wander down to the placid River Serein, visit the twelfth-century Church of St. Martin (the saint who has attracted such devotion in France that many towns, villages and hamlets bear his name and an enormous number of churches are dedicated to him). St. Martin is the Roman soldier who, according to tradition, sliced his cloak in half to give one portion to a shivering beggar – who then appeared to Martin in a dream wearing the cloak, manifest as Jesus Christ. Martin is the patron of horsemen, so horseshoes will be seen at the church – they were also often votive offerings by pilgrims, for, although Chablis is not right on the great medieval pilgrim routes that cross France to Spain and St. James (Santiago) of Compostella, it is not far away and there are numerous great abbey churches, notably that of Avallon.

A half day in Chablis will reward the traveller with architectural charm, varied countryside and a clear sight of the finest *Grand Cru* vineyards that peer down into the town's centre. A cellar tasting at the establishment of M. Fèvre, a superb grower, in rue Jacques Rathier, will offer a cool tasting of a range of Chablis wines; the shop of M. Soulié in the Place Général de Gaulle stocks many wines, local specialities, cheese and vinous accessories, and just into rue Auxerroise the well-stocked wine shop of Le Cercle Brennus has a tempting selection of Chablis, mostly from the estates of M. Laroche.

Explore the surrounding villages, though sadly they are not well served for eating and staying. For midday refreshment the villages of Beine (Le Relais de Chablis) and Ligny le Châtel (l'Auberge du Bief) have restaurants providing *'un déjeuner'* capable of creating the memories necessary for the fulfilment of holidays spent touring the wine region of France. For staying the night, it is possible to find good and modest accommodation in Auxerre, Tonnerre or Joigny (though for the speedy traveller there is a motel at motorway exit Auxerre Nord).

WHAT ARE THE WINES OF CHABLIS LIKE?

Firstly, it must be clearly established that we are discussing genuine Chablis, produced under the tight French laws of *Appellation Contrôlée*, and not in any way including the many abusers of the Chablis name around the world. The most discreditable is the legal 'non-protection' of the Chablis title in the U.S.A., where American dry white wines are often labelled 'Chablis' entirely for commercial purposes to take advantage of the name to which they have no right and the wines may not even contain any Chardonnay. Other countries offend as well.

Chablis, as produced in the true Chablis region, comes as four *Appellation Contrôlées*: Chablis Grand Cru; Chablis Premier Cru; Chablis and Petit Chablis. These four A.O.C.s of Chablis produce only white wines.

Never compare Chablis directly with the other white Burgundies, for the latter do not have the similar steely dryness and delicious balanced acidity, wrapped into a strength of flavour, that develops in the best-quantity Chablis after two or three years of bottle age following the vintage. These qualities will obviously be found in varying degrees amongst the seven *Grand Cru* vineyards, through the eleven *Premier Cru* vineyards, down to the straight Chablis and smaller production of Petit Chablis.

It will be observed that older Chablis does not gain depth of colour nor does it maderise to any extent. Any 'Chablis' that is a deep yellow-gold colour is unlikely to be genuine.

Something like half the Chablis produced is bought in bulk by the Burgundy shippers of Beaune and Nuits St. Georges for bottling under their own label. Although most of these shippers will treat their Chablis purchases with great respect and bottle without fault, it is sensible for the interested wine amateur to buy Chablis wines that have been bottled in Chablis by a leading producer – either a grower or a *négociant*.

Chablis vintages fluctuate in quantity more than their Burgundy cousins further south in the Côte d'Or. This causes greater movement of market prices, both up and down. Prices for Chablis in 1978/79 shot upwards and have not taken a downward turn following an abundant crop in 1982. None the less the value of top Chablis wines remains excellent, at the time of writing. Chablis is once more a fashionable wine – one might cynically say because many customers in export markets can fearlessly ask for it without fear of mispronouncing the name. It is to be enjoyed either as an apéritif, or an ideal companion to many luncheon and dinner dishes, meat and poultry as well as fish.

Descriptions of Chablis can only be generalisations but you should none the less look for a few essentials: a clear pale colour in the centre of the glass with the outer rings of tone being a greenish-yellow hue in young wines. Once the wine has been two or three years in bottle its hue acquires a wheaten colour, but never accept a Chablis with darkness to it. The smell should be clean, showing a direct, uncomplicated dryness with a slight yeastiness. The flavours, dependent on the particular A.O.C. and the wine's age, will naturally vary, but look for a firm, dry taste, which fills out in the mouth without undue acidity. The best wines will have an attractive balance of initial aggression that tempers down into a fine smoothness.

CHABLIS TODAY

Vinification methods and equipment have improved considerably since the middle of the 1960s to a point where well-trained growers and *négociants* (but alas, by no means all) can rescue a potentially poor harvest and produce a vintage of adequate standard that would formerly have been totally lost. The most noticeable change in the last fifteen years has been the cellar modernisation by the successful growers/*négociants* – nowadays the Chablis producers regularly offer acceptable qualities but of course the number of great vintages has not increased. Making great Chablis is a costly struggle, as will be clear if you stand in front of the hills of the *Grand Cru* and note the steepness of the vineyards.

Vineyard ownership is split amongst many *vignerons* and *rentiers* (tenants). Only the dedicated growers will be successful because of the poor-quality soil and unreliable weather conditions, which can bring late frosts and hail, and destroy within hours the entire year's crop. The harvest is never safe until it is picked, pressed and in the *cuves* (fermentation vats), during which time *chaptalisation* is necessary (see page 38). Throughout the vinification, care is needed not to spoil both the character and the delicate balance that make up the unique charm of Chablis. Making Chablis is therefore and probably always will be a struggle, rewarded on average only five years in every ten with a decent vintage.

Wines of the Chablis *Appellation* must reach a minimum of 10° of alcohol content. If you buy do not allow these to get too old, although some from the *Grand Cru* vineyards can age for up to ten years if carefully stored, and also if they come from a vintage renowned for youthful power, such as 1979 and 1981. In general, in order to appreciate Chablis allow for two to four years' maturation in bottle, when the wines will show their distinction more vividly, having lost their initial sharpness.

THE WINES

Grand Cru – **the finest growths.**   Looking out from the main square of Chablis across the little River Serein, a tributary of the Yonne, you can see the seven *Grand Cru* vineyards joined together in a row facing south: Vaudésir, Preuses, Les Clos, Grenouilles, Bougros, Valmur and Blanchots.

Only in fine vintages will the wines of these vineyards be sold under their own names; otherwise they will be declassified at the decision of the grower down to *Premier Cru* Chablis, or even to straight Chablis. The laws of A.O.C. require *Grands Crus* to reach 11°, and, as with all Chablis *Appellations*, the only grape permitted is the Chardonnay (its local name is the Beaunois).

Other grape varieties such as Sacy and Aligoté can be found in the Chablis region, but they can only be used for Bourgogne Grand Ordinaire and Bourgogne Aligoté respectively.

The flavour of *Grand Cru* Chablis is special in every respect. For colour, observe the green hues glinting among the golden shadows; smell the wine slowly by inhaling the bouquet after agitating the glass. The taste fills out in the mouth and spreads across the tongue, leaving a delicate aroma within the mouth.

The wines are bottled roughly a year after the vintage, but need another three or four years to reach their peak. The variations in taste between products of the different vineyards can be left to the local experts; however, in my experience, Grenouilles and Les Clos have given me the finest bottles.

Chablis Premier Cru – second growths. The River Serein is the key to Chablis. You can see the *Grand Cru* vineyards virtually jostling the town. Now to explore the second most important *Appellation* of Chablis, the *Premier Cru* (although in fact, in this context the description does not mean 'first' at all, but 'second').

Until 1967 there were 22 vineyards scattered along the left and right banks of the Serein that were entitled to *Premier Cru* status. This number was reduced to eleven to avoid confusion and the following names were retained as the best known. On the south side of the Serein: Beauroy, Côte de Lechet*, Vaillons, Melinots, Montmains*, Vosgros. On the north side of the Serein: Fourchaume*, Montée de Tonnerre, Monts de Milieu*, Vaucoupin, Les Fourneaux.

It must be understood that vineyard holdings here are very fragmented, leaving little chance for a grower to produce a wine from one single patch of vineyard in any quantity, so this amalgamation of names became necessary to keep to the commercial sales requirements. In fact, the grower retains the right to use the old vineyard name (French logic), or the new name, or even just *'Premier Cru'*, without the vineyard name.

In offering a tasting description it seems churlish to criticise *Premier Cru* wines at all, though I feel obliged to indicate some essential difference in quality against the *Grand Cru*. Half a degree of alcohol actually separates them and from the slight reduction to a minimum of 10.5° results the lesser weight of flavour and more muted highlights. Perhaps, once fully developed, the *Grand Cru* wines will yield more subtlety but this will depend on the tasting undertaken by the individual and his or her tasting memory.

Chablis. The average production of Chablis in good vintages is nearly 1¼ million bottles – by comparison with production in

---

* Means vineyards producing wines usually seen on the export market.

other wine regions, this is not much to satisfy the world. As the vineyard area is spread throughout the villages of the nearby countryside and along the exit roads towards Auxerre, Tonnerre and Maligny, it is striking that the vine has not maintained itself as a predominant feature of the landscape as it was in former times.

The wines that are sold as straight A.O.C. Chablis never carry a vineyard name, but this is not important. Fragmented vineyard ownership causes growers to blend their wines, possibly from several sites. This blending is beneficial, as it enables the grower or shipper to balance his *cuvées* (vattings), which certainly improve when individual merits can be transferred to the wines lying in wood or vat prior to bottling.

When tasting or drinking straight Chablis, it is probable that the first impression registered will be the taste buds' quick reaction to the acidity of the wine when young. Normally this will break down with bottle age, but the wine beginner will be aware of the sharpness of the tongue and around the teeth when tasting such youthful wines. This acidity is essential for Chablis and, as long as it is not excessive, the character of Chablis needs it, if the wine is to remain firm and upright in taste. Without its natural acidity, Chablis will not live and improve. Do not be afraid of the acidity: it harmonises well with the concentrated cold steel backbone of true Chablis.

The appearance of Chablis has provoked many attempts to describe its colour. You will find it paler and greener, without the slight hay yellow of the *Grand Cru* and *Premier Cru* wines. But, as with them, the taste is gripping and definite.

To find the main villages of the region responsible for the wines of the straight Chablis *Appellation* visit Maligny, Beine, Lignorelles, Chemilly and Bertu. Tastings and cellar visits are possible, but you may have to push yourself forward and certainly either speak French or try to do so (see Appendix 1).

The wines for the *Appellation* Chablis are produced exclusively from the Chardonnay grape. They are generally more acidic and less fruity than those wines entitled to the A.O.C.s *Grand Cru* and *Premier Cru*, which makes them ideal for drinking in their two years of life.

Petit Chablis.   Petit Chablis is not a large *Appellation*. It is about a ninth the size of Chablis and has never been well known outside France. The impression of Petit Chablis is probably false in that many consumers believe that the word *'Petit'* is slightly denigrating, implying an inferior wine. This is not so, although it must be agreed that it is less fine than the *Appellation* 'Chablis' and the higher growths.

Several growers are now replanting land never under vines since the disaster of phylloxera in the last part of the nineteenth century, hoping that the growing world demand for Chablis wine may thereby be satisfied in the less affluent countries which can enjoy the clean, crisp wines of Petit Chablis. A change of title to 'Chablis Villages' has been proposed and this, if adopted, would be welcomed by exporters.

The permitted area for planting vines around Chablis can hardly be increased without a fall in quality and though replanting of old vineyards potentially increases production, we cannot expect to see production move much higher. Should Chablis face abundant vintages in the mid-1980s we may see a period of stable prices, which in time will bring back Chablis drinkers lost by the high prices of 1978/79/81. Chablis does not have a fashionable image, as do, for example, Sancerre or Pouilly Blanc Fumé, but should the wines ever benefit by protection from label abuse round the world, then there could be an explosion of demand for Chablis which would be unlikely to benefit the existing customer.

OTHER WINES

Bourgogne Aligoté. A small amount of the Aligoté grape is grown around Chablis to make a delicious wine for regular drinking. It is dry, with the chalky flavour coming from the Chablis soil. It is different from the Côte d'Or Aligoté, with a marked added crispness and light, dancing taste. It is rarely exported, except by the firm of Lamblin of Maligny, who offer it under the label 'Grand Blanc de Lamblin'.

Bourgogne Grand Ordinaire. The white grape variety Sacy is also found in the outer Chablis region, but the wine made from it is entitled only to the *Appellation* Bourgogne Grande Ordinaire. Mostly consumed locally and not often seen on its own, it is sometimes purchased by shippers to contribute a sprightliness to a blend for the A.O.C. Bourgogne Grande Ordinaire.

Seen locally but rarely exported, the following are the remaining wines of Lower Burgundy:

Irancy. A red wine grown on slopes behind the village of Irancy. It needs much age and is only successful in hot summers. It has a somewhat heavy style.

Coulanges-la-Vineuse. A red wine somewhat similar to Irancy.

St. Bris-le-Vineux. A white wine made from the Sauvignon grape (used in the Loire for Sancerre and Pouilly Fumé). It has a distinctive dry, aromatic bouquet with a light flavour.

Avallon. White and red wines from the valleys of the Rivers Cure and the Cousin are made, though only the red wines have any real reputation. They are supposedly quite vigorous.

Auxerre. A local, pleasant and dry rosé from this once large vineyard may be found in the restaurants.

All the above vineyard areas are on the south side of the A6 – that is, in the direction of Auxerre on the other side from Chablis. To the east of Chablis the town of Tonnerre maintains a few vineyards in the Armançon valley. These produce both red and white wines, the quality of which is entirely unknown to me. If anyone knows of them, I shall be delighted to learn more.

Côte de Nuits

The enthusiastic amateur of wine travelling through the Côte d'Or has opportunities of tasting in each village where facilities are available, but do beware of roadside *dégustations* aimed solely at selling. Only rarely will quality or value be available at such places. The local restaurants offer a reasonable selection of wines from the Côte d'Or but prices are expensive for visitors and vintages will appear young. In the region the youth of the wine may not detract from your pleasure in sampling it but the bottle age essential for full and mature enjoyment will not have taken place. However, some of the simple region *Appellations* will often surprise visitors by their quality and they need not be costly.

NUITS ST. GEORGES

The actual boundary of the Côte de Nuits is clearly marked at Corgoloin, an ugly village, the home of famous marble quarries that, with their neighbour at Comblanchien, spread a thin white film of dust over everything in the vicinity. However, the country route through Pernand Vergelesses (see page 89) and over to the Hautes Côtes de Nuits is very pleasant. Follow the signs to Nuits St. Georges. On this route you emerge through the trees high above Nuits St. Georges and the quarries are bypassed. Between the quarries and Nuits St. Georges on RN74 the wine interest begins at Prémeaux. This is a mere village but the wines made here are entitled to be called Nuits St. Georges.

If you go to Nuits St. Georges on the main Beaune–Dijon road (RN74), thereby saving a little time, notice the vineyards on your left. Virtually all the village and vineyard *Appellations* will be on the left-hand side as you are going north, as this road is an ancient route, originally laid to mark the limit of the fine wines from the hillside. To the right there are many vines extending towards the River Saône and the railway line, but, with rare exceptions, they will be allowed only generic A.O.C.s. The aristocrats are on the other side, to your left.

Nuits St. Georges is the main town and commercial centre of the Côte de Nuits, home of many *commissionnaires en vins* and the location of the cellars of several well-known shippers. The most important vineyards in Nuits St. Georges lie to the south of the town, adjacent to the main road between Nuits and the village of Prémeaux. The character of true and genuine Nuits St. Georges is typified by a firmness and depth of flavour. It is usually better for keeping. Perhaps the wines of Nuits lack the noble finesse and breeding so obvious in their immediate neighbours to the north but many excellent medium-priced wines can be found and enjoyed.

The *Appellation* area of Nuits St. Georges covers 375 hectares (926 acres). It is the effective beginning of the Côte de Nuits, although further down the road the smaller villages of Prissey, Comblanchien and Corgoloin join with Brochon and Fixin to make the wine for the Côte de Nuits Villages A.O.C.s.

The town of Nuits (the 'St. Georges' was added in 1892) should be visited for the fine church of St. Symphorien and the Roman remains to the east at Les Bolards. The road through Nuits is always busy and quite narrow, with shippers' establishments close to the pavement. So park the car and walk through the side streets leading off the square; the change of atmosphere will mark the amazing tranquillity and timelessness that is so much the essence of the Côte d'Or.

HOSPICE DE NUITS ST. GEORGES

This hospice was founded in 1692. The first actual building was the Salle St. Laurent, followed by the Salle Ste. Madeleine and the Salle St. Étienne. After the French Revolution the administration passed from the Augustinian religious order to the Mayor of Nuits, at which time two sisters were appointed to nurse the thirty-six patients living there. During the nineteenth century special attention was paid to tubercular patients and further extensions were made; as tuberculosis was gradually conquered, the administration of the Hospice changed direction towards geriatric care and it now takes special pride in its peaceful facilities for the old and poor. The Hospice started with twelve beds in 1692; it now maintains 166.

As with the more famous Hospices de Beaune, the Hospice de Nuits has been aided by gifts of vineyards from local benefactors, whose names are given to the various cuvées of the Hospice wines. It was only in 1938 that the Hospice administration first decided to offer the wines of their 1937 vintage at auction. The encouraging results of the first auction were interrupted by World War II and only in 1962 did the foundation again auction its wines to the public. By the time of the 1975 vintage there were fifteen *cuvées* of Nuits St. Georges named and offered in this way. The wines are offered by *pièce* (the Burgundian cask, holding approximately 228 litres or 50.2

gallons), and these fifteen wines were offered in twenty-six lots, a total of seventy-two *pièces*. It is possible to find these different Nuits St. Georges wines on lists, although they are much less well known than the *cuvées* of the Hospices de Beaune.

Wines from the following classified vineyards will be regularly available: Les Procès, Les Pruliers, Les Porrets, Les Vaucrains, Les St. Georges, Les Perdrix, Clos des Corvées, Clos de la Maréchale. The following growers/*négociants'* labels are widely distributed: J. C. Boisset, Cruse, F. Chauvenet, J. Faiveley, Geisweiler Domaine Gouges, Grivelet, Cusset, Labouré-Roi, Liger-Belair, Lupé Cholet, Morin, Jules Belin (at Prémeaux), Charles Viénot (at Prémeaux) and Moillard.

VOSNE ROMANÉE

When you leave Nuits St. Georges, drive north (still on the RN74) and immediately look out for the sign to Vosne Romanée indicated to the left; it is preferable to take the first vineyard road but, if you do miss the turning, don't worry as there are two other roads leading to the village slightly further along.

In order to study the Vosne Romanée vineyards, which surround the village like jewels, you should have as detailed a map as possible, because it is essential to appreciate the way in which the vineyards fit together and are placed on the ground. If you can, buy the Larmat map of the Côte de Nuits. This costs about 30 francs and you will usually be able to get it in Nuits St. Georges or Beaune. It will look good framed when you get home after your visit, too.

The atmosphere of Vosne Romanée is charged with associations, memories and expectations – heady stuff for the wine lover. A short stop in one of the lanes will help you to recognise the importance of where you are and to concentrate your mind on this village in which five world-famous vineyards are clustered together, together with several others that are also renowned. Very little ordinary wine is made in this area because the geography, climate and soil combine in the most favourable way to assist the growers in their noble task of maintaining a reputation formed over centuries.

The village of Vosne Romanée has suffered on many occasions in the past from marauding foreign troops and it was largely rebuilt following the local fighting during the 1870–71 Franco-Prussian War. The hundred-year-old buildings now show signs of dilapidation and, as in most villages, little is being done to rebuild or repair them.

The atmosphere of Vosne Romanée is essentially private. The tourist trade is somewhat grudgingly welcomed because the streets are narrow and the increased traffic of sightseers interrupts the routines of a working village. But explore and register the place – it will linger in your mind when you try the wines.

Romanée Conti Wines.   In Vosne Romanée one must begin at the top of the quality scale and consider the vineyards belonging to the Domaine de la Romanée Conti. They are the sole owners of the site of Romanée Conti (1.8 hectares, 4.4 acres), which has an average production of a mere twenty to twenty-five *pièces* per vintage.

The highest praise has often been accorded to Romanée Conti wines and they have an expansive, deep richness, in which both bouquet and flavour seem to melt into each other, achieving a harmony of power that is quite unique. They can, of course, live for many years, and in a mature condition the price they fetch is forbidding. However, a few bottles purchased in their youth would be a reasonable treat for a serious collector – this is the kind of 'wine investment' that is well worth making.

Since the earliest records of the thirteenth century this tiny vineyard has changed ownership only nine times. The other vineyard solely owned by the Domaine de la Romanée Conti is that of La Tâche (6.02 hectares, 14.8 acres); in commercial terms it yields a more important crop. In the wines of a La Tâche there is a tendency to a more velvety flavour, smoother but lighter than is generally found in Romanée Conti.

Other great vineyards of Vosne Romanée are shared by several proprietors, the Domaine de la Romanée Conti remaining among the largest holders.

La Romanée (0.83 hectares, 2.05 acres) is entirely owned by Liger-Belair, shippers of Nuits St. Georges.

Romanée St. Vivant (9.54 hectares, 23.5 acres) has a section owned by the Domaine de la Romanée Conti, who still possess a few rows of vines planted before phylloxera struck and consequently ninety years old. These aged vines yield little but their grapes play a significant part as regards quality. In my experience the perfume of the bouquet contributes to the majesty of this growth – it has a lingering backtaste that consolidates the balance. The wine of Romanée St. Vivant will be found under several labels but I would need to be very certain of its provenance before laying out my money for it and would only buy such a wine from a supplier who had my confidence. The reason for this attitude is simple: it is possible for a poor vintage to be put on sale, the supplier hoping that the mere name 'Romanée St. Vivant' will do the selling – and cloud the judgement of the buyer. I mention this particularly with reference to Romanée St. Vivant because I was recently offered – and rejected – a parcel of a usually sound vintage that disgraced the name of this noble wine and its *Appellation*. (Yet I am sure someone will buy it.)

Richebourg (7.99 hectares, 19.7 acres). The wines of Richebourg possibly present a great variety of styles than the other top growths of Vosne Romanée as this vineyard has the greatest number of proprietors. For this reason, too, Richebourg is more widely sold and will be seen on lists throughout Europe and the U.S.A. In peak condition the wine is robust, very generous and uncomplicated, which may sound slightly derogatory, but is not meant to. Class and style capture the imagination in a Richebourg, leaving no doubt that a fine wine has graced your palate.

Other vineyards of outstanding merit include:

Les Grands Echézeaux (9.14 hectares, 22.5 acres). This vineyard is on the south side of the minor road leading towards Vougeot. The wines possess a great elegance and delicacy that can be unrivalled, yet they are less well known than they deserve, due to their name, supposedly 'difficult' for anyone speaking English. Remember them, however, for an opportunity may arise when a bargain presents itself; then you will appreciate Grands Echézeaux as a truly *'grand vin'*.

Les Echézeaux (30.08 hectares, 74.3 acres). This consists of a group of eleven vineyards, partly surrounding Les Grands Echézeaux and on the upper side of the road. Great bottles of Les Echézeaux are not always to be found synonymous with the wine's name and a good vintage date. This is certainly a label that requires some advice before you pay a vast sum for a bottle in a restaurant. The wine can be a little tough in youth and will usually benefit from a reasonable amount of bottle age before consumption. In 1984, for example, I would try to drink the 1973 or 1976 vintages. This is a very good *Appellation* for laying down in the right vintage because it is the least expensive of all the great growths of Vosne Romanée, perhaps both because of the difficulty in export markets as regards the name and because people may suppose it to be somehow inferior to Les Grands Echézeaux.

Growers in Vosne Romanée whose labels are widely distributed are: Domaine de la Romanée Conti, Domaine Gros, Domaine René Engel, Domaine Henri Lamarche, Domaine Charles Noëllat.

CLOS DE VOUGEOT

Continuing along the vineyard road N74 out of Vosne Romanée, you will find that the land undulates considerably, thereby providing many small *combes* (coombs) and *coteaux* (small hillsides). The brushland of the upper *côte* seems close, as the vineyards give way to the trees that grow thickly here and

Clos de Vougeot, centre for the Chevaliers du Tastevin

continue upwards to the top of the *côte* and over on to the plateau.

It is a landscape that varies very much in detail, so drive slowly. As soon as the road descends gently you will see opening out before you on the right the prospect of the Clos de Vougeot and its vineyards, which stretches right down to the road (RN74). The road goes directly behind the buildings of the Clos de Vougeot.

The history of the Clos de Vougeot begins in the early twelfth century when the Cistercians were first given the land, which remained in their possession until the French Revolution in 1789. During this period this establishment gained a high reputation for its wine, employing what we might describe as a public relations promotion programme. Judicious gifts of wine to the 'right people' – the higher ranks of the clergy, the more influential nobility, rich merchants and the smarter court favourites – drew attention to the quality of Clos de Vougeot. It was a subtle strategy that had great success. The public invariably respond to 'church produce' even when, as with the Cistercians of the Clos de Vougeot, the makers of the wine did not officially drink it themselves.

After the Revolution the Clos de Vougeot property was confiscated by the State and auctioned off to one buyer, a M. Focard. Until 1889 the vineyard remained in single ownership but was subsequently auctioned off in lots. Since that time an increasing number of growers have owned portions of the Clos de Vougeot vineyard, which has been further divided by the French laws of inheritance which, according to the Code Napoléon, generally mean that property must be divided among all the immediate heirs; as a result vineyard holdings are often split up into plots of no more than miniature allotment size. It is very doubtful if a situation whereby eighty growers with varying shares of a 50-hectare (123.5-acre) site can produce a uniformly exciting wine. It is, none the less a great status symbol to own a portion of such a vineyard.

Today's owners may be divided and categorised as follows:

1. The *négociants* of Beaune and Nuits St. Georges, who add
    some glamour to their ordinary business by owning a plot
    here. Some familiar names can be found among these
    proprietors such as Morin Père et Fils, Pierre Ponnelle,
    Faiveley, La Reine Pédauque, Champy Père et Fils and
    Jaboulet-Vercherre.
2. The small grower, usually part of a larger *domaine*, who
    may sell in bulk to a *négociant* without himself undertaking
    the bottling of the wine. Hence you will see Clos de
    Vougeot on many shippers' lists, but they themselves do
    not necessarily own any vines in the Clos de Vougeot vine-
    yard. They buy them in from the *négociant* or even the
    small-scale owner.

I fear that before the stricter days of the enforcement of the
A.O.C. regulations, many wines called 'Clos de Vougeot' were
sold throughout the world when their provenance was doubtful.
At its best the wine is lush, highly developed, with plenty of
stamina and a sinewy quality.

Because of the great reputation of Clos de Vougeot – a
Burgundy name every drinker knows – it is essential to buy this
wine only from a source on which you can wholeheartedly rely.
Each grower has vines of different ages, so he may pick at
different times and promote a slow or fast fermentation
according to what he thinks is best. The variation of wines that
may be truthfully called 'Clos de Vougeot' is therefore
enormous. The good shipper, buying from a selection of these
assorted lots, will blend them so that the result is a harmonious,
balanced wine, typical of Clos de Vougeot overall and resulting
from the shipper's selection of wines that are both good and able
to be satisfactorily married in his individual blend. This is
where his skill and reputation make his name of ultimate
significance and importance on the wine's label.

In former centuries it is said that the monks divided the wines
from the Clos de Vougeot into three qualities relative to their
geographical position. Wines from the lower ground by the
road were called 'Cuvée des Moines'; from the highly favoured
middle ground 'Cuvée des Rois', and from the high ground
'Cuvée des Papes'. Stendhal relates the emotional reaction of
the French towards Clos de Vougeot when telling of a M.
Bisson, a colonel in the Revolution, who, marching his troops
past the vineyard, required them to 'present arms', while the
regimental band was blazing away. This grand gesture was
later imitated by Maréchal MacMahon (1808–93) who became
Duc de Magenta and owned sizeable estates in Chassagne
Montrachet.

The Clos de Vougeot is one of the most famous buildings in Burgundy and you must stop to look at it. Notice how low its walls are, so as to permit an enlarged roof area. In former times the monks were very short of fresh water and this typical Cistercian building, which looks as if it is pushed into the ground, acted as a type of waterbutt for every shower of rain; the drainage from the roofs enabled the maximum quantity of rainwater to be caught and retained. (A further account of its history can be found on page 17, which deals with the wine order, the Chevaliers du Tastevin.)

The Clos de Vougeot was first wall-enclosed in the twelfth century, but the buildings today date from the sixteenth century when the Cistercians rebuilt them around the original and ancient press house and cellar. This is an essential sight for any Burgundy lover; the giant beam press, rather like a prehistoric animal, is something to gaze at in awe – from it have come wines that made the reputation of the Côte de Nuits.

Visiting hours are from 9 a.m. to 11.45 a.m., and from 2 p.m. to 5.45 p.m. It is closed from 20 December to 5 January.

VOUGEOT

Vougeot is really dominated by the Clos and the remaining vineyard land left over for the village is small. The village itself is of little interest, though the wines of three vineyards will be seen quite regularly on more extensive lists and are well worth trying: Clos de la Perrière, Cras and Clos du Prieuré. The Domaine Bertagna is probably the best-known estate dealing in these Vougeot wines and the Beaune shipper, Pierre Ponnelle, has gained an excellent reputation for his Domaine du Prieuré.

My advice to the traveller following this route would be to visit the Clos de Vougeot, then drive down to the main road in order to look back up the hill and view the Clos and the surrounding vineyards from a distance. The building and its vineyard epitomise Burgundy for so many people throughout the world that you should register as many impressions as possible of the whole comparatively small area. At the main road there is a tasting establishment, La Grande Cave, which may make a welcome stopping place to visit.

Return up the lane by the Clos, past the entrance to the junction and then turn right. Facing you is the great vineyard, Le Musigny, split into two by a track – altogether it totals only 10 hectares (24.7 acres). Ownership is fragmented into ten proprietors, of whom the most renowned is Comte Georges de Vogüé, whose cellarmaster, Roumier, also owns vines in Chambolle and Morey.

CHAMBOLLE MUSIGNY

Le Musigny demonstrates the real glory of red Burgundy. When I read what has been written over the last two centuries, I note descriptions of the wine as unique for its delicacy, richness of bouquet and majestic finesse. I would not disagree – although its price means that this is a wine for special occasions.

It is worth stopping on the road at this stage and noting the contrast of the scrubland above the vineyard with the poor-looking soil of the vineyard itself: it is incredible to think how the worth of the land changes from the intensely valuable ground of the production area to the useless rubble, merely feet away.

The village of Chambolle Musigny can be reached by this secondary road, with the charmingly named vineyard, Les Amoureuses, on the right side, facing that of Le Musigny. Further on towards the village crossroads vineyards to the left and right decline in status, apart from that of Les Charmes. On reaching the junction, turn left up into Chambolle Musigny, for this little village, which is unusually situated above the main vineyards, has some most attractive houses and a church noted for some good paintings of saints. If you want a stopping place, I can recommend leaving the village by the road so as to enjoy the wooded ravines and rocky, calm countryside.

The wines of Chambolle Musigny are highly rated by such members of the trade as are able to taste them regularly. Somehow they possess an underlying weight and nobility of flavour that is perhaps unexpected by those who are primarily impressed by their exquisite bouquet and soft fruitiness. I find them fascinating wines, with the particular merit of yielding a range of very attractive smells. But, of course, they are not cheap.

A wine that is less expensive and that illustrates the divergence of Burgundies correctly offered under the A.O.C. Bourgogne Rouge may be found by visitors to the area: this is the Bourgogne Rouge of Comte Georges de Voguë. It must, by A.O.C. laws, come from the vineyards in the *domaine* of Comte Georges de Voguë in Chambolle Musigny. It is often listed at the modest restaurant attached to the Samotel at Beaune, route d'Autun. Its elegance and style are remarkable. Bear in mind that Bourgogne Rouge can sometimes also be a declassified A.O.C. from a higher category. In average vintages this protects the good name of the *domaine*, but still gives the purchaser an agreeable experience. So look for the *domaine*'s name on the label, not merely the name of the wine. Remember too, that *domaines* cannot buy wine in; they can only sell their own produce.

The Côte de Nuits tour continues by taking the road out of Chambolle Musigny towards Morey St. Denis. A most important vineyard is to be seen on the left of the road – Bonnes Mares, which is entitled to its own A.O.C. as one of the first growths of Burgundy. The unusual name has never been fully explained, though several suggestions have been made. The one I find most appealing comes from shipper, merchant and writer Christopher Fielden, who suggests that 'It comes from the old Burgundian verb *marer*, to plough; the vineyard was well tended.' Whatever the name's origin, the wines of Bonnes Mares, which are available from several growers and shippers, please fastidious palates, for they are rich and firm, combining both depth and charm. They develop slowly over the years, reaching a peak at least ten years after their vintage. A Bonnes Mares 1959 of Comte Georges de Vogüe tasted recently ranks among the finest red Burgundies I have tried. The Bonnes Mares site overlaps Morey St. Denis, though this is unimportant because the wine does not need to mention its village on the label.

MOREY ST. DENIS

Leaving Bonnes Mares behind, the road leads to the top of Morey St. Denis. Here there is the well-known Clos de Tart vineyard on the left. This has remained in the hands of a single owner since 1932 – the Mommessin family of Mâcon, world famous for their Mâconnais and Beaujolais wines. Clos de Tart is widely listed and reaches high prices but its style will only appeal to those Burgundy drinkers who prefer pale wines of fruity youth, as this particular wine does not seem to have the longevity of its neighbours.

The wines of Morey St. Denis often represent excellent value as against the highly inflated prices of some of the masterpieces previously mentioned (which too frequently simply sell to those with a lot of money who merely want to 'drink the label'). The character of the Morey wines is quite definite: power combined with a magnificent bouquet. A number of vineyards have become sufficiently well known (apart from Clos de Tart) in increasing the reputation of Morey St. Denis. These are: Clos St. Denis, Clos de la Roche, Clos des Lambrays and Les Sorbets. Before the delimitation of village *Appellations*, the wines from Morey were often sold as Gevrey or Chambolle, so until recently they never had the chance to build up their own reputation. Apart from growers such as Roumier, whose Clos de la Bussière has a regular following, a recommendation can be made for those wines purchased by Bouchard Père et Fils and Chanson Père et Fils. Since writing the first edition of this book, the name of Jacques Seysses of Domaine Dujac, has become well known among serious students of fine Burgundy. Striking an individual note on vinification, without later fining and filtration, he has provoked much debate. Only the personal judgement of drinkers can decide whether the richness and intensity of his wines matches the style needed for the occasion. The Domaine Dujac is widely listed in the very best restaurants in France and the U.S.

GEVREY CHAMBERTIN

After Morey St. Denis the vineyard road is clearly signposted 'Circuit des Vins de la Côte de Nuits'. It goes towards Gevrey Chambertin, whose boundary is crossed soon after leaving Morey. The road descends towards Gevrey Chambertin, where there is an impressive line-up of first-growth vineyards on both sides. Stop and look about if you have time.

On the left there are: Latricières Chambertin, le Chambertin, Chambertin Clos de Bèze, Mazis Chambertin, and Ruchottes Chambertin (above Mazis). On the right: Mazoyères Chambertin (now sold as Charmes), Charmes Chambertin, Griotte Chambertin and Chapelle Chambertin.

The ownership of these vineyards is extremely varied but in my experience they are capable of giving exquisite bottles. The Charmes Chambertin has the largest production and will consequently be found more often. If one offers some general tasting notes, they must be taken in the correct context – one person's tasting opportunities can vary greatly from those of others and writers sometimes risk generalisations about wines without giving the circumstances in which they tried them, sometimes in somewhat flattering and luxurious circumstances. But to me the wines of the Chambertin first-growth vineyards have a rather heavier and more aggressive character that is most appealing if they accompany the traditionally rich Burgundian cuisine.

The folklore surrounding Napoleon claims that Chambertin was his daily wine during his days of supreme power. Some Paris merchants took an ignoble business advantage of this after the Retreat from Moscow in 1812 by offering 'Chambertin, *Rétour de Moscou*', though it had probably never travelled further than the Halle aux Vins (the daily market for cheap table wine distribution in Paris that catered for wholesale distribution before the growth of shops and, eventually, supermarkets). As if having Napoleon for its champion was not enough, Gevrey Chambertin was also the home of Gaston Roupnel, the poet who spoke of Burgundy with the same fervour as did the rather more eminent poet, Frédéric Mistral, about Provence. One example of his lyricism about Gevrey Chambertin will suffice: 'It blends grace and vigour. It unites firmness with power, finesse and delicious differing qualities that compress together an admirable synthesis of unique generosity and of complete virtue.'

The history attached to the Chambertin Clos de Bèze and le Chambertin dates back to the seventh and thirteenth centuries respectively, though both vineyards are now discussed together. They lie next to each other and, such are the irrationalities of the labelling laws, the wine from the Clos de Bèze can be called Chambertin, but not the other way round. Apparently the success of the monks at the Bèze vineyard caused a M. Bertin to buy the adjacent field; in time its name was compressed from Champ de Bertin to Chambertin. From the thirteenth century until the French Revolution the Clos de Bèze remained in the same ownership, the Chapter of Langres. The name of Chambertin was, however, placed firmly on the commercial market by a M. Jobert, who, at the beginning of the nineteenth century, introduced it throughout the courts of Western Europe by a leasing arrangement that he made on very advantageous terms.

There is now a first-class restaurant here, the Rôtisserie de Chambertin, where the finest growths can be drunk amid sumptuous surroundings, although the cost of a visit is high. Up behind Gevrey there is a special, ancient part of the village, leading into the Combe de Lavaux; here the vineyards of St. Jacques and Cazetiers produce wines of the higher order. In this part of the village I recommend a visit to the Château (it is open from 9.15 a.m. (10.15 on Sundays) until noon and from 2 p.m. to 5 p.m.; there is no charge). It originated in the tenth century and was restored in the thirteenth; it has many features of local interest. If you have time, follow the D31 out of the village through the Combe de Lavaux and climb towards and across the plateau for about 6 kilometres (3.75 miles); the views are beautiful.

Apart from the vineyards already mentioned, Gevrey Chambertin has some very fine second-growth wines which will probably be seen regularly. They are: La Combe aux Moines, Les Champeaux, La Petite Chapelle, and Varoilles.

There is a second section of the village of Gevrey Chambertin called Les Baraques astride the main road RN74. Against all the usual labelling rules the classified vineyards of Gevrey stretch over the road on to the plain and down to the railway. Among the sites the wine of Clos de la Justice, belonging to Pierre Bourée, is one of my first memories of fine Burgundy. It seems to have dropped out from lists in recent years, possibly being a casualty of the direct trade, the increasing 'grower-to-consumer' market that has become a nuisance to trade distributors.

Throughout Gevrey Chambertin there are many distinguished growers. Those whose names are often seen on lists include: Armand Rousseau, Drouhin-Laroze, Camus, Bourée, Domaine Varoilles. Among the *négociants*, Pierre Ponnelle, Faiveley and Joseph Drouhin always have excellent wines from the village and its great growths.

BROCHON AND FIXIN

To leave Gevrey Chambertin follow the usual signs marked Brochon and Fixin but be careful to take the higher road from the top end of the village so as to see the vineyards from the most favourable vantage points. You soon arrive at Brochon. The village has no *Appellation Contrôlée* of its own and its wines are used in the blend for Côte de Nuits Villages on account of their vigorous character. A few vineyards abutting on Gevrey Chambertin are entitled to the latter name. A modern château, built in 1900 by the poet, Stephen Liégeard, has been converted into the local school. This writer is better remembered, however, for creating the tag 'Côte d'Azur' in one of his works, when referring to a section of the Mediterranean French coast.

The next village, Fixin, also has its place in the Napoleon legend. Captain Noisot of the Imperial Guard was overcome by the departure of Napoleon from Fontainebleau in 1815 after the Hundred Days, when he bade a dramatic farewell to the Imperial Guard in what is now known as the *Cour des Adieux*. Noisot purchased land in Fixin and in 1846 created a park, named for him, with a statue by the sculptor Rude 'The Awakening of Napoleon'. As a piece of sculpture it is charged with emotion, though the figure of Napoleon is perhaps somewhat bovine to non-French eyes. Near the Parc Noisot is a small museum containing some souvenirs of the imperial campaigns. Visits can be made between 9 a.m. and 12.30 p.m. and from 1.30 p.m. to 7 p.m.

As a wine village Fixin has now regained some of its stature from the time when it was the leading vineyard site of the former Côte de Dijon. After the dreadful phylloxera plague of the 1870s Fixin wines were rarely used under the village label as they were bought for blending with those of Gevrey Chambertin and others. However, even during this period, the vineyards Clos de la Perrière and Clos du Chapitre always retained their reputation, so keeping the name of Fixin from disappearing entirely.

Fixin gained its village A.O.C. in 1936, whereafter its fortunes began to improve. By the 1960s it could claim to have recovered, with *négociants* taking an interest in listing Fixin as a lower priced Côte de Nuits wine. The attraction of Fixin wines seems to be their special depth of flavour, showing an earthy taste that will appeal to the Burgundy drinkers who favour the larger and coarser styles. I have enjoyed a number of Fixin wines and, in addition to the two vineyards mentioned earlier, I suggest readers look out for those of the Clos Napoléon, La Mazière and Les Hervelets. At La Mazière the proprietor, Dr Marion, had some very old vines of the early 1900s. His wine reflected this age by its dark colour, intense bouquet and sturdy backbone, reaching perfection in both the 1971 and 1972 vintages. Apparently a lot of replanting was done in the late 1960s and it will now take a few years for the wine made from these younger vines to gain this concentrated taste. The same grower has a small, highly prized section of the Chambertin site. A rare white Fixin is now produced.

Fixin is the last village officially within the Côte de Nuits. The vineyard road does not come to a definite end but enters the suburban mass of Dijon. Unless you wish to visit this city, however, there are two other places of wine interest to see.

MARSANNAY LA CÔTE

Marsannay, which suffered from the economic depression after World War I, has fought back by producing the only decent rosé wine of the Côte d'Or. The Pinot Noir grape skins are allowed only a short contact with the must, just enough to tint the juice a lively pink. It is one of the few rosé wines that can be taken seriously. This is not intended to be derogatory to other rosés, but the rosé of Marsannay has the depth to withstand the heavy sauces of the Burgundian kitchen and its fruitiness enchants the palate. Most of the production comes from the Cave Co-operative and from Clair Daü, one of the most famous *domaines* in Burgundy, who have vineyards in all the favoured sites of the Côte de Nuits.

CHENÔVE

There was a time when Chenôve enjoyed a fine reputation for two red wine vineyards, Clos du Roi and Clos du Chapitre. The sole attraction now is the Cuverie des Ducs de Bourgogne where the magnificent presses of the fifteenth century can be seen, one called 'Big Maggie' after Marguerite, Duchesse de Bourgogne. It is said that she had a 'great capacity' – for wine or what? The press was able, it is said, to produce sufficient wine to fill up to a hundred *pièces* at a single pressing. (Visits from 8 a.m. until noon, and from 2 p.m. until 7 p.m.)

The Corton Circuit

The best route to take for this mini-tour follows the old road towards Dijon, going over the autoroute. Immediately one sees vines on either side of the road. The Corton circuit starts

immediately after Chorey-lès-Beaune, to the left. A signpost to
the village of Aloxe Corton is clearly marked. This minor road
has the appearance of a private drive because it is extremely
straight and at the end a really beautiful house comes in sight,
the Château de Corton, now the trading home of a mail-order
house, André Frères. The village has many examples of the
attractive Burgundian roofs. There is a great deal of warmth
about the architecture and the village reflects this, particularly
during the late evening in high summer when the sun's rays are
strong and some of the buildings actually seem even more
glowingly yellow. As the houses in Aloxe include several that
were built for merchants, they have a superiority of architecture
that is not found in the more workmanlike villages nearby.

Aloxe Corton lies at the foot of the Montagne de Corton and
behind the village the ground rises quite steeply, the vineyards
climbing upwards towards the wooded, tree-topped hill. The
great vineyard, Corton Charlemagne, extends in a great loop
round this hill towards the village of Pernand but the
production of the Pernand vineyard here, while it actually
traverses the boundary of Pernand, is entitled to the Corton
Charlemagne *Appellation*. The ownership of the vineyard is split
between several large owners, of whom Louis Latour and
Jaboulet-Vercherre are the best known, as well as other small
vignerons, who, until recently, would sell their wines to the
Beaune shippers; now they increasingly reserve their stocks for
their own bottling and for sale to private customers. The
Corton Charlemagne wines are exclusively white with a style
rich in flavour yet fully dry. The description may appear
contradictory but the sense of their richness can be noticed
when they age and their taste becomes all-pervading.

Apart from the Charlemagne, the finest wines from the
leading vineyards of Aloxe Corton are red. Notice should be
taken of Le Corton, which produces the most exciting and long-
lived bottles of all Côte de Beaune wines. They are rightly
described as '*vins de garde*' (wines to keep) because they do have
extraordinary longevity – up to twenty-five years if in sound
cellarage. The immediate flavour of Corton may appear slightly
thick and earthy but time erases the hardness and replaces it
with a refinement that is quite classical and a style extremely
close to the finest Côte de Nuits wines.

The interesting situation of the Le Corton vineyard shows
how geographical location and position in relation to the sun
play such an important part. Le Corton is a long, thin strip of
vineyard beneath the Bois de Corton where the northern end
will enjoy early sunshine and the southern end will see much
more of the late and, possibly, drier hours of daylight. There is a
curiosity of labelling in Corton in that the *Premier Cru* vineyards

are preceded simply by the word 'Corton'. It is only the second-growth vineyards that are preceded by the full village title of 'Aloxe Corton'.

Wines from the following classified vineyards will be regularly available: Le Corton, Clos du Roi, Vigne au Saint, Les Marechaudes and Les Bressandes. Growers/*négociants*' labels widely distributed include: Louis Latour, Prince de Mérode, Chanson Père et Fils and Tollot Beaut.

PERNAND VERGELESSES

Because the important vineyards sweeping round from the Bois de Corton are entitled to the *Appellation* 'Corton', the production of both red and white Pernand Vergelesses is limited and the wines are not well known. The reds are big wines without the grace of Corton or the softness of Savigny but they are rewarding after some years in bottle, having power and a noticeable *goût de terroir* – a flavour of the particular vineyard soil. An example of this is the excellent vineyard wine, Île de Vergelesses, offered by Louis Latour.

White wines labelled under the village name must be produced from the Chardonnay grape, which (page 28) is the sole white grape for both village and single vineyard wines of the Côte d'Or. There is a distinct similarity between the whites of Pernand and the neighbouring Corton Charlemagne, but they are difficult to find: the *négociant* Marcel Amance in Santenay offers an excellent Pernand white in good vintages which he buys from a grower who also has vines in the Corton Charlemagne vineyard. The other permitted white grape variety, the Aligoté (page 29) can only be sold under its original *Appellation* 'Aligoté' but, grown in Pernand it does produce some of the best qualities of its kind. If you are interested in contrasts in living, then on this circuit, contemplate the modern autoroute A6 from a point of vantage in the ancient village of Pernand Vergelesses. The two worlds do not meet.

Wines from the following classified vineyards will be regularly available: Île de Vergelesses and Les Fichots. Growers/*négociants*' labels that are widely distributed are: Dubrueil Père et Fils, Bonneau du Mattray, Rapet Père et Fils. No visits appear to be possible at the time of writing.

SAVIGNY-LÈS-BEAUNE

To the visitor arriving via the autoroute A6 into the Côte d'Or, Savigny is the first village to be seen as the motorway drops down sharply from the plateau towards Beaune. Savigny-lès-Beaune shelters in the valley below on the left with its main vineyards spreading out from the valley, round the hill up to Pernand Vergelesses, towards the front of Aloxe Corton near the RN74 and down towards Beaune, where the Savigny vineyards abruptly end at the motorway. On this part of the motorway several shippers have built new fermentation cellars, including Chanson Père et Fils. They wished to be nearer to their two exclusive vineyard holdings in the Beaune/Savigny area because in the past they had problems with fermentation during an abundant harvest. The grapes would begin to ferment while *en route* to their more distant cellars in the hot weather, something which is wholly undesirable.

Savigny-lès-Beaune is a pretty village with a very reasonable hotel, l'Ouvrée, which is suitable as a Côte d'Or base. The proprietor, M. Petitjean, owns several plots of vines in Savigny and his wine is naturally sold in the restaurant.

The majority of wines from Savigny-lès-Beaune are red with a soft and fragrant smell. If drunk when younger than their more famous neighbours they can be good. Savigny is an excellent example of a sound medium-priced wine, as against the often inflated value of more fashionable villages.

A small quantity of white wine is made and, again, the Aligoté of this village is much sought after by the shippers for their blends. Wines from the following classified vineyards will be regularly available: Aux Vergelesses, Marconnets, La Dominode, Aux Guettes and Les Lavières.

CHOREY-LÈS-BEAUNE AND LADOIX SERRIGNY

Ladoix Serrigny is the first, or, as you may prefer, the last of the villages of the Côte de Beaune. This double hamlet is entitled to its own village label but the best sites are permitted the *Appellation* Aloxe Corton for the red wines and Corton Charlemagne for the whites. This is a quirk of geography

View of La Rochepot above the Côte de Beaune

because the sites are simply an extension of the prime sites of Aloxe Corton, continuing across the east face of the slopes of the Bois de Corton. Chorey-lès-Beaune also enjoys a village *Appellation*, but its wines are usually used as part of shippers' blends for Côte de Beaune Villages. As they are grown entirely on the plain, they cannot claim to have outstanding characteristics, but they are usually firm, ideal for blending as a unifying force with more fragrant wines.

Growers/*négociants*' labels of Chorey-lès-Beaune that are widely distributed are: Arnoux Père et Fils (visits accepted), J. Germain at the Château de Chorey and R. Voarick.

Routes in the Beaune and the Côte de Beaune Vineyards

In former times the wines of Beaune were probably synonymous with Burgundy in general as far as most foreigners were concerned. The Beaune vineyard itself has the greatest 'surface' or area under vines of all the Burgundy region round about, although it does not produce as much wine as, for example, Pommard. But it is easy to understand why the wines became so well known: not only were they within easy reach of the town of Beaune itself, but other named vineyards, which are now producing wines under their own labels, such as Pernand and Savigny, were probably in the past all sold simply as 'Beaune', an easy name for many export markets to pronounce too. (It should be stressed that, in this context, references to Beaune are solely to the vineyard and the wines, not to the town, the culture, or anything else.)

Although you can make a rapid trip by taking the car in the direction of the Montagne de Beaune and Bouze-lès-Beaune to get a panoramic view of the vineyards, it may be of interest for those with more time to know that the excursion into the Beaune vineyards is perfectly practicable on foot, even if you start by walking from Beaune itself. Leave the road and follow the vineyard tracks, wander about for a couple of hours and you will have a wonderful impression of being among the vines and seeing 'where it all happens' while at the same time walking off any excesses of Burgundian fare and wine. It is perfectly permissible to follow vineyard tracks but don't walk between the rows of vines and remember to greet anyone you meet. The Burgundians will usually be delighted to see anyone taking an active interest in the vineyard.

In following this itinerary visitors must expect to see the contrast between modern and old France. From quite near to Beaune itself one can look down on the medieval town, encircled by ramparts, which, like most French towns today, has in recent years spread out into a sprawl of modern development. In the modern part of Beaune (the suburbs) many of the major wine houses now have their installations for bottling and actually making the wine (in the *cuveries* or press houses) and it is from there that about half a dozen of the important shippers will despatch their wine. Should anyone be inclined to despise these modern installations, it must be stressed that by moving part of their premises in this way, the shippers have enabled the centre of the town to remain free from juggernaut lorries and general traffic snarl-ups which the narrow streets cannot cope with.

It is worth reminding the reader that the *Appellation* 'Beaune' is not the same as Côte de Beaune or Côte de Beaune Villages (see page 136). The importance of distinguishing in one's mind between the three names lies in the fact that they are three distinct areas and are hence productions in their own right. Consequently they have separate places in the wine social order.

The actual wines of the *Appellation* Beaune are attractive for the beginner learning about Burgundy, for they are fullish in style and easy to drink. While there is a tiny amount of white wine, the vast majority of Beaune is red. In tracing the history of the style of wines made from these ancient vineyards we find a tradition of vinification to create wines of a light fruitiness without the same stamina as some of the more lordly villages of the Côte de Nuits.

Records show that Beaune wines were essentially trading wines that became well known in Paris and, later, in London as generally representing Burgundy. By the nature of the vineyard's soil and exposed position it is quite natural for this style and character to be accorded to the wines today but it may be a little unfair because some outstanding wines are produced: I would cite the tiny vineyard owned by Bouchard Père et Fils of the Vigne de l'Enfant Jésus and there are others. Nevertheless it is possible to postulate the theory that when, after the French Revolution at the end of the eighteenth century, the domination of the vineyards by the religious establishments and great estates of the aristocracy came to an end, it was the Beaune vineyards that were first purchased by the established shippers in the nineteenth century for more rapid commercialisation, simply because of the quality of the wine produced. The name 'Beaune' was easy to sell, the style of wine was easily drinkable. The same applies today, especially in export markets where some buyers still hesitate before names that are seemingly difficult to pronounce.

When I am faced with a lengthy so-styled 'gastronomic' meal, I am always cheered to see the wines of Beaune served, because they blend well with the richer and more succulent foods and cause no difficulty with digestion. Oddly enough the more demanding wines of the Côte d'Or, with their concentrated flavours, can be more easily enjoyed – and talked about – when they accompany somewhat simpler dishes. To me, Beaune wines have an uninhibited and slightly casual approach and, with the benefit of a few years' sales experience dealing with the wines of Beaune, I can say that, now that all these wines are bottled in the region of production, the demand for Beaune has fallen away. Why? Possibly because customers think that another wine with a more complicated-sounding name will be of superior quality. Or maybe the 'Beaunes' of yesteryear were not truly representative of the region, although low in price. The majority of regular Burgundy drinkers now seem to prefer the greater stamina of Corton, Pommard and Volnay. But may I put in a strong plea for people to forget all the nasty Beaunes they may have drunk – many of which were bottled in Britain – and return once more to these charming helpful wines. Also, the price for Beaune is never quite as high as that of the wines mentioned above. On a restaurant list this is a distinct advantage.

The town of Beaune has been the wine trade centre of the Côte d'Or since the fourteenth century. The region has been variously owned – by the church and sundry religious orders, the nobility, the Crown, even the Knights of Malta, until the change of land ownership following the Revolution when the proprietors were dispossessed and the vineyards auctioned. The vineyards did not, however, pass to the real peasant worker because they were purchased by both the small growers then in existence and the merchants. During the nineteenth century and the first half of this century the shippers have gradually acquired more vineyards and, in the immediate Beaune area, they have become the principal owners: for example, Drouhin, Chanson and Bouchard Père et Fils.

HOSPICES DE BEAUNE

The wines referred to and labelled as 'Hospices de Beaune' are those that belong to this institution, which consists of the Hôtel-Dieu de Beaune and the Hospice de la Charité, also in the town. In 1443 the Chancellor of Burgundy, Nicolas Rolin, and his wife, Guigonne de Salins, endowed the Hospices and their statues may be seen in the courtyard. Rolin was responsible for many of the great architectural glories of Burgundy and the curious and richly decorated Hôtel-Dieu was built with the aid of Flemish craftsmen, which accounts for its unusually styled roof. The Dames Hospitalières, a Flemish nursing order, still run the institution, but accommodation is now in more modern buildings.

VISITING THE HÔTEL-DIEU

Guided tours take visitors round the Hôtel-Dieu and about an hour should be allowed for this. You should in particular look at and appreciate the remarkably patterned roof, also the Salle des Pauvres, with the curtained bunk-type beds, so arranged that the patients could see the celebration of Mass at the end of the huge room (it was occupied until comparatively recently); there is also the pharmacy, the enormous and beautiful kitchen, and – worth detailed study – the great work of art, Roger van der Weiden's 'Last Judgement'. A guide may offer visitors a magnifying glass so as to see the meticulous care with which tiny plants, such as a strawberry, are depicted in this masterpiece.

What the Wines Are

The generations of benefactors of the Hôtel-Dieu and Hospice de la Charité endowed these institutions with vineyards, either as gifts or legacies, and it became an established tradition for the wines from these plots to bear the names of the original owners. All the wines come from the Côte de Beaune, except one lot from the Côte de Nuits. Since 1859 they have been sold at a public auction in all but exceptionally bad years when a private sale disposes of them. The auctions attract great publicity and buyers from all over the world; the Trois Glorieuses (see page 22) during the third weekend in November coincide with them so Beaune is full of restaurateurs, persons in the public eye and a variety of journalists, all present for the occasion.

Today, the *cuvées* or vattings of the wines sold at the Hospices de Beaune consist of twenty-three *cuvées* of red wines, nine of white, plus some brandies and *marc* (see page 48). They range from Meursault in the south to Mazis Chambertin in the north. The Hospices labels state the village from which the wine comes, the vineyard, and the *cuvée*. In some instances wines from two or three vineyards in the same village may be blended together to make up a *cuvée*, and when this happens the wine will bear the A.O.C. of the village. The *cuvée*, as has previously been stated, bears the name of the original benefactor, donor of either the plot or vineyard, or a particular vatting and usually the name of an individual is as well known as the A.O.C. Some memorial!

The Hospices are no longer solely financed by the sale of wines, the cost of modern medicine now exceeding even the most expensive of wines, but the vineyards do contribute substantially to their upkeep. Until recent years the prices fetched at the Hospices' auction were a strong indication of

Mounting casks (pièces) for storage

market prices of Burgundy in general. However, since 1970, with the inflationary spiral of fine wines, the Hospices wines have tended to surpass in price the maximum that shippers find they are able to obtain for their own wines, even those bearing the same A.O.C.s. Those who, understandably, think of Beaune wines as red, should remember that it is usually a white wine, Corton Charlemagne, Cuvée François de Salins, that fetches the highest price.

The wines are offered at auction in lots of casks (*pièces*), the Burgundian cask of oak, which contains approximately 300 bottles or 228 litres (50.2 gallons). In the 1981 sale 429 *pièces* were listed, the sizes of the separate lots varying between five and nine *pièces* per lot. Buyers have to remove the *pièces* from the Hospices cellars within one month of sale. Henceforth the bottling of the contents of the casks becomes the sole responsibility of the purchaser. It will, therefore, be appreciated that wines from the same vineyards and indeed from the same named *cuvée* may vary considerably, according to who does the bottling. For this reason it is as unwise to make generalisations about the Hospices wines as it is to generalise about Burgundy: the ultimate quality and style can be determined only by whoever buys and handles it.

It is worth stressing that, although the visitor may find much of interest to see in Beaune at the time of the sale, admission to the auction in the covered market is by ticket only and, because space is limited, places are taken by the wine trade and their guests. Accommodation in hotels is very difficult to find at sale time and all restaurants and shops are crowded, so it is unwise to count on seeing the auction or to stay in Beaune in late November. A brief look around is all that will be possible – and be sure you have your next place of stay definitely booked.

HOSPICES DE BEAUNE WINES

The wines are:

WHITE

Cuvée	Village	Vineyard
François de Salins	Corton	Charlemagne
Bahezre de Lanlay	Meursault	Charmes
Loppin	Meursault	Les Criots
Baudot	Meursault	Genevrières
Philippe le Bon	Meursault	Genevrières
Jehan Humblot	Meursault	Poruzots
		Grand Charrons
Goreau	Meursault	Poruzots
		Les Pitres
		Les Cras
Albert Grivault	Meursault	Charmes
Paul Chanson	Corton	Vergennes

RED

Charlotte Dumay	Corton	Les Bressandes
		Clos du Roi
Docteur Peste	Corton	Bressandes
		Chaumes-et-Voirosses
		Clos du Roi
		Fietre
		Les Grèves
Rameau-Lamarosse	Pernand Vergelesses	Les Basses
Arthur Girard	Savigny	Marconnet
		Les Peuillets
Forneret	Savigny	Vergelesses
		Gravains
Fouquerand	Savigny	Vergelesses
		Les Talmettes
		Gravains
		Serpentières
Hugues et Louis Betault	Beaune	Grèves
		Mignotte
		Aigrots
		Sizies
		Vignes Franches
Maurice Drouhin	Beaune	Avaux
		Boucherottes
		Champimonts
		Les Grèves
Dames Hospitalières	Beaune	Bressandes
		Mignotte
		Aigrots
		Teurons
		Grèves

Nicolas Rolin	Beaune	Centvignes
		Grèves
		En Genet
Brunet	Beaune	Teurons
		Bressandes
		Mignotte
		Centvignes
Guigonne de Salins	Beaune	Bressandes
		En Senrey
		Champimont
Rosseau-Deslandes	Beaune	Centvignes
		Montrevenots
		Mignotte
		Avaux
Dames de la Charité	Pommard	Épenots
		Noizons
		Arvelets
		Rugiens
Blondeau	Volnay	Champans
		Taille Pieds
		Ronceret
		En l'Ormeau
General Muteau	Volnay	Village
		Carelle
		Cailleret
		Fremiet
		Taille Pieds
Gauvin	Volnay	Santenots
		Pitures
Jehan de Massol	Volnay	Santenots
Lebelin	Monthélie	Duresses
Boillot	Auxey Duresses	Duresses
Madeleine Collignon	Mazis	Chambertin
Clos des Avaux	Beaune	Avaux

POMMARD

A visit here can extend the tour of the Beaune vineyards or, if you have sufficient time, make a pleasant tour on its own. Leave the *boulevard* or circling road that goes around Beaune and aim south on the RN74. Soon after the Samotel (where you can stay with a vineyard view from your window), take the right-hand road in the fork, N73, signposted 'Autun'; this leads directly to Pommard itself. As you turn off at this junction the Pommard vineyards are on the left and right of the road. Ahead, take the way through a chain of villages with names that mean much to the lover of wine – Volnay, Monthélie, Auxey Duresses, St. Romain. You can return later by the road that leads off from Monthélie to Meursault, through Puligny Montrachet, Chassagne Montrachet and as far as Santenay, from which point you can return to Beaune via Chagny on the RN74.

Just before you reach Pommard itself, on rising ground to the right, note the vineyard of Les Épenots (or Épenaux – the spelling can vary). On the left here is the fine-looking Château de Pommard, a single, enclosed vineyard, a rarity in Burgundy, owned by M. Laplanche. Visitors can be received here.

Pommard itself is a quiet little wine village; it lives by and, literally, on wine, every house being that of a *vigneron* or small proprietor, with cellars beneath. Walk about the little streets and observe the unusual-shaped belfry on the church. Pommard gets its name from Pomona, the presiding Roman deity of gardens and fruits (hence the word *pomme* meaning apple). The wine was a favourite of the great nineteenth-century author, Victor Hugo. Look out over the vineyards: the important site, Les Rugiens, often seen on wine lists, is on the slightly higher ground between Pommard and its neighbour, Volnay. Turn right in the centre of the village and you can get to the equally famous Clos de la Commaraine vineyard, now owned by the well-known shipper Jaboulet-Vercherre.

Pommard at its best is a fine wine, with a deep, brilliant colour, a gracious fruitiness and a softness that develops charmingly as the wine ages; fine Pommard of a great year can be a tremendous wine but it is not all that easy to find these days. Indeed, Pommard's reputation has, in the opinion of many Europeans, suffered as the result of the enormous popularity of its wines in North America; this market has been prepared to pay prices higher than those of any other export markets in order to get the wine it finds so acceptable.

In consequence, not merely does the American buyer now risk not always getting a wine of quality in accordance with the high price paid, but the demand for this wine – it too has a name easy for Anglo-Saxons to say with assurance, another factor of by no means negligible importance – has tempted some *vignerons* to cash in on its popularity. There has, therefore, been some forcing up of production to the maximum permitted by the A.O.C. regulations. In other words the vineyards have been strained so as to make as much wine (and to produce as much money) as can possibly be achieved legally. This has naturally led to a lowering of quality standards. So choose your source of Pommard with special care!

Wines from the following classified vineyards are usually readily available: Château de Pommard, Clos de la Commaraine, Les Épenots (Épenaux), Les Rugiens, Les Pézerolles, Clos Micot and Les Arvelets. Growers/*négociants* whose labels will be featured on many export lists include

Jaboulet-Vercherre, Château de Pommard, Comte Armand, Billardet-Gonnet and Clerget.

VOLNAY

After you leave Pommard the road climbs somewhat to Volnay and then runs in front of the village. The larger proportion of vineyards is on the left here, so that there is a sensational view of them down to the main road, RN74. In fact Volnay is an excellent place to stop, look and reflect – preferably when you have recently enjoyed a fine bottle of its wine. Survey the vineyards, whether you do so on a sunny day or when the clouds huddle over the Côte d'Or and showers make you glad to be able to get back into the car. Those of us who enjoy wine for its essential simplicity – the pleasure it gives immediately – will claim the enjoyment of fine Burgundy as a stimulus to the tired intellect; we are gratefully drawn into the study of this wonderful wine. So pause on the Volnay road, look back to Pommard, follow the vineyard round and eventually go on to Meursault. Wine lovers are truly fortunate! Even if you have not always felt this, you will do so when you stop for a moment's thought and silent expression of gratitude in the midst of the birthplaces of so many wonderful wines.

Because it stands a little high, Volnay is exposed to the elements and there is a real danger of frost. This can sometimes be counteracted by smudge pots, placed strategically among the vines; the pots are filled with charcoal and lit when the temperature drops to danger point. They send out a general warmth in their vicinity so that the frost cannot bite and destroy the vegetation. Perhaps because of this exposure, the wines of Volnay are markedly delicate, sometimes even fragile, but note the subtle flavours of good Volnay too, underlying the delicacy. Take time. Let the Volnay breathe and develop in the glass – swing the wine round a little to encourage this – and then concentrate on the wine as you drink it. Volnays are also good 'beginners' wines' because they please immediately with their soft but insinuating bouquet and light fruitiness that leads on to a deeper velvetiness and lasting charm.

Volnay wines are red, yet there is an odd contradiction in the A.O.C. laws concerning the white wines which are also grown there, for these, adjacent to Meursault as they are, are entitled to the A.O.C. Meursault, not Volnay. In the same bureaucratic way the best red wines that are the product of vineyards inside the Meursault-defined area are entitled to the label Volnay Santenots or, if of a slightly lower quality, the label may bear the straight name Volnay.

Wines from the following vineyards are usually widely available: Clos des Angles, Caillerets, Champans, Clos des

Chênes, Fremiets, Pousse d'Or, Santenots (in Meursault) and Chevrets. Growers/*négociants* whose labels are widely distributed include: Domaine de la Pousse d'Or, Henri Boillot, Bernard Delagrange, Bouchard Père et Fils, Le Cellier Volnaysien and Marquis d'Angerville.

MONTHÉLIE

After leaving Volnay the road forks: the left-hand route goes to Meursault and the right-hand to Monthélie, Auxey Duresses and St. Romain. Allow about forty-five minutes if you are going to see Monthélie and the other villages or, if you haven't time, go straight to Meursault.

Monthélie is a tiny, ancient village, tucked around the corner of the hill on high ground. It is said to get more sun than any other village in the Côte d'Or and it is naturally sheltered. But the soil is very poor indeed – no other crop apart from vines can be grown successfully. Note too, the 'quilted' effect on the roofs of the houses produced by the overlapping tiles with their scalloped edges – these are true 'old Burgundy'.

Monthélie's wines are 97 per cent red; the white is a rarity although it is made. Formerly the wines of Monthélie would be used for the *cuvées* of Volnay and even of Pommard when these wines, on account of their well-known names, were the big-selling Burgundies. But Monthélie got its own *Appellation* in 1937 and since then has been making strenuous efforst to get its wines known and estimated in their own right. They are generally light in style and very fragrant, with a clear, brilliant red colour and are, of course, usually less expensive than other Côte de Beaune wines. Monthélie is also able to be drunk and enjoyed when, by wine standards, it is still quite young: some Monthélies are delicious as early as three or four years after their vintages. The white wines, which are never seen on export lists, should certainly be sampled in the village café. Monthélie is now becoming widely available on wine lists and the wines of the classified vineyard, Les Champs Fuilliot, can sometimes also be found.

The growers' co-operative can receive visitors to their premises, Les Caves de Monthélie, from Easter until November. Robert & Bernard de Suremain, at the Château de Monthélie, can also receive visitors, even group parties if an appointment is made at Les Caves de Monthélie.

AUXEY DURESSES

Continuing along the right-hand fork past Monthélie, the next village, Auxey Duresses, is set in the entrance to a gorge dominated by the Mont Meliam; the principal vineyards lie to the right on ground that is too high to produce great wines. A vineyard that is too exposed will suffer more from variations in the weather than one that is slightly sheltered. Hence the finest growths come from sites that are half or two-thirds of the way up a slope, the rising ground behind both offering some protection and providing drainage.

A parenthesis on pronunciation: you will find Burgundians in the countryside pronouncing the 'x' of their villages as a true 'x' and not as a double 's', which is the way another Frenchman would say the word. The village names to which this applies in the Côte d'Or are: Fixin, Aloxe Corton and Auxey Duresses, also Buxy in the Côte Chalonnaise. So, when you use these names, decide whether you want to use 'French' pronunciation and say 'Fissin', 'Aloss', 'Aussey', 'Bussy' or to opt for the clearer Burgundian sound pronouncing the 'x' hard.

Auxey Duresses produces around 70 per cent red and 30 per cent white wine. Both of these can now be found on the British market; they represent real value and have not so far had their prices inflated by fashion. The red is not appreciably different from Monthélie – in other words, it is a small-scale Volnay. The white wines are capable of rivalling those of Meursault, without quite developing the depth of flavour that is associated with this famous name. The white wines give an agreeable feel of power and their bouquet is delightful but I recommend selecting young vintages, because these wines have a tendency to 'maderise' or discolour quickly, their peak point being comparatively short.

The wines and the gastronomy of the region can be sampled, without an undue deficit to the pocket, at La Cremaillère in Auxey Duresses.

Wines will usually be available from the classified vineyards of Les Duresses, Clos du Moulin des Moines, and special mention should also be made of the Cuvée Boillot, of the Hospices de Beaune, which is usually an excellent red wine. Growers/*négociants* whose labels are widely distributed are: J. Leroy (co-distributor of the Domaine de la Romanée Conti), and Michel Prunier.

The Caveau Communal in Auxey may be visited by appointment.

ST. ROMAIN

St. Romain received its full *Appellation* as recently as 1967. Since then, the grower Roland Thévenin has promoted the wines to great effect. (He is also an important grower in Puligny Montrachet.)

The vineyards of St. Romain are the highest of the whole Côte d'Or. On this exposed position the Chardonnay grape, producing white wine, is more hardy than the Pinot Noir that makes the reds. When drunk young and fresh, St. Romain Blanc is an excellent, fresh, apéritif wine; the red can be an ideal prelude to something greater.

Growers/*négociants* whose labels are widely distributed are: Roland Thévenin, also Chanson, the Beaune shippers, who promote this *Appellation*.

There are no individual vineyards worth recording in this area but, because of St. Romain's position, it is worth stopping and walking up to the panoramic lookout on the summit of the mountain, which is reached by a path on the right, past farm buildings. On a clear day it is possible to see over the Mâconnais and Beaujolais to the south and, eastwards, across the Saône valley to the Alps.

If you return to Auxey Duresses and follow the RN73 out of the village, the road climbs on to the Hautes Côtes de Beaune towards Nolay and Autun. If you are travelling by this route there is a country road which reaches Santenay at the far end of the Côtes de Beaune, via Nolay and Paris l'Hôpital, crossing over the RN6 (the old Lyon–Paris road). If there is time to spare on this excursion, detours should certainly be made to see the still-impressive establishment of Cluny (though much smaller now than in its great days) and the superb Romanesque cathedral at Autun.

Meursault and La Côte des Blancs

At the road fork outside Volnay, the left-hand road runs down into Meursault, which can also be reached from the main RN74. This is an essential trip for anyone hoping to learn about white Burgundy.

Meursault is not a village, but it is also not quite a town. However, it is the capital of La Côte de Blancs, which, besides Meursault, includes the villages of Blagny, Puligny Montrachet and Chassagne Montrachet. From these villages come the finest dry white wines in the world. The atmosphere of the place, evocative of dry white wines, is strongest in Meursault. The straggly, narrow streets are abundantly adorned with growers' signs, cellars are almost everywhere under your feet. It is a romantic capital, with a little square around the fourteenth-century St. Nicholas Church with its elegant spire (a mini-model of the cathedral at Autun). Opposite the church is the Restaurant Mère Daugier, which specialises in hot pâté. If you stay there, however, remember to ask for a room at the rear, for at the front you will be nearer to the church bells than is good for the ears. Meursault is also well organised for camping sites and provides for the devotees of motels. Part of the festivities of the Hospices de Beaune auction weekend, Les Trois Glorieuses, take place in Meursault, where luncheon on the last day, La Paulée, is held (page 25).

The ruins of the twelfth-century Hôpital de Meursault sit on the other side of the main road (RN74) at the junction with the village road. This building was originally a lepers' hospital and hence was outside the town, but many years ago it fell into disuse, although it is still a handsome ruin. Notice the original level of the entrance to the hospital, which is now several feet below the main road – an example of how some buildings can sink and roads be built up.

Meursault is known uniquely for white wines, as previously mentioned. The small amount of red wine that is grown on the Volnay boundary is entitled to the Volnay *Appellation*. Within the Meursault *Appellation* area are included some of the wines from the hamlet of Blagny, which sits higher up the slope between Meursault and Puligny. The adjectives used by generations of wine writers to indicate the flavour of Meursault have perhaps helped towards belief in the alleged pomposity of the wine trade, but it really is difficult to describe such a complex family of wines. If one has to generalise one begins to be, at best, enthusiastic – as I am! Meursault is distinctive in bouquet, combining the smell of light fruit and developing traces of nuttiness as it ages. It starts life quite pale in colour, almost a pale lemon, but this soon changes to a full, definite yellow. The taste contrasts richness with an essential dryness; balance between these two is vital for fine Meursault, which is the fullest and most rounded of all the Côte d'Or white wines. What Meursault may sometimes lack is the class and refinement of the wines that come from the great Puligny vineyards (pages 104–5). The best wines of Meursault will last five or six years but do not be tempted to keep it for too long. There is nothing worse than old white Burgundy, in my opinion – its greatness as a superb white wine lies in the combination of its freshness and its maturity.

Between the town of Meursault and the boundary of Puligny there are five vineyards, each of international repute. It would be reasonable, therefore, to suppose that as each of these vineyards produces wines that are different as regards shades of character, it should be possible to offer individual tasting notes about each of them. But, as will have been appreciated by the reader who has understood the complexity of Burgundy wines, there are no single proprietors of these vineyards. Therefore each owner will make a wine slightly different from that of his neighbour: he will pick the grapes at a different time; he may vinify in a slightly individual way; he – or the shipper who buys from him – will handle the wines according to the 'style of the house'. So, in the end, it really is impossible to make the sort of generalisations that enable the student of wine to put a definite tag on wines such as these. (This is another reason why buyers of Burgundy should try to become acquainted with the house style of even a few – whether from shippers or growers.)

It may, nevertheless, be of slight help if some basic characteristics are mentioned. The vineyard Goutte d'Or will usually possess the fullest character, contrary to that of Les Charmes, where bouquet and fruit balance linger more gently. Those of Les Perrières and Poruzots have a more aggressive style, leaving the vineyard of Les Genevrières to unite all these charming subtleties. But it is also fair to say that I could probably find exceptions to all these descriptions in the cellars of any Meursault shipper at any time.

Wines from the following classified vineyards will be regularly available: Perrières, Charmes, Genevrières, Poruzots, Goutte d'Or and Chevalières.

Visits can be made to the Château de Meursault (now owned by Patriarche Père et Fils of Beaune) and there are tastings in their fourteenth-century cellars. There are daily tastings (except on Fridays) at the Maison de Meursault (a growers' co-operative), and also tastings at Le Manoir Murisaltien.

The following growers can receive visits by appointment: Jean Ampeau Germain, Raymond Javillier, Domaine Comte Lafond, Ch. Genot Boulanger, Réné Monnier, Domaine Jacques Prieur and Ropiteau Frères.

PULIGNY MONTRACHET

There is a vineyard circuit road linking Meursault with Puligny without rejoining the main road, from which it is evident that the vines of both villages are separated only by tracks. *En route* you see Blagny on the heights to the right: its wines are divided between Meursault and Puligny Montrachet, but the village name is attached, such as Meursault Blagny, or Puligny Montrachet Blagny. A small amount of red wine is produced and this is merely named Puligny.

Puligny, when seen in the sun, has a sense of retained heat and strength; it often seems to be empty of people, but they are there somewhere. They produce, within this vineyard's limits, the greatest selection of dry white wines in the world. The hotel restaurant Le Montrachet, in the centre of the village, is ideal for the traveller.

Taking the road signposted 'Chassagne Montrachet et Santenay', you climb gently out of the village, passing vineyards on the left and right, up towards the sites of Les Bienvenues, Bâtard Montrachet, Le Montrachet and Chevalier Montrachet. These great vineyards follow each other up the hill, divided only by the Chassagne road, which turns sharply left between Bâtard Montrachet and Le Montrachet. The latter is on the right: both have walled enclosures and doorways into the vineyard. This is an essential stopping point from which to feast the eyes and senses on the glorious view.

Looking back towards Meursault down a track road you will see other great vineyards of Puligny – Les Caillerets, Les Folatières, Clos de la Garenne and Champ Canet on the middle ground to the left and, easing down towards the village, Les Pucelles, Calvoillon, Les Referts and Les Combettes. So all the great white wines are produced on this gentle hillside in a long line but vary according to their position *vis-à-vis* the sun and the changes in soil substance, which will affect and influence the final wines in many subtle ways. Le Montrachet and Bâtard Montrachet straddle the boundary with Chassagne, but these vineyards have their own *Appellation*, so there is no question of having to determine whether the wine is produced in Puligny or Chassagne.

Le Montrachet is unique – the concentration of fruit and acidity produces flavours of exquisite refinement, capable of living beyond reasonable age, as white wines are usually rated. In 1975 a Grand Montrachet 1929 of Baron Thénard was found to be a perfect old gentleman – polite, stimulated by company but quickly tired. (Forgive the emotional language – it arises from passion, not pomposity. I shall never forget that bottle!)

Sufficient homage having been paid to Le Montrachet, you take the road that descends to the RN6, the old Lyon–Paris highway before the autoroute A6 existed. In fact, the last vineyard on the left before the RN6 is Criots Bâtard Montrachet (tiny, approximately 2 hectares, or 5 acres in extent) where the whole vineyard lies within Chassagne and is consequently separated from the village and the rest of Chassagne vineyards by the main road. I have noticed that Criots Bâtard Montrachet does not age as graciously as the rest of Chevalier, Bâtard, Bienvenue and Le Montrachet, and it would drink at its best some three or four years after the vintage; however, in the rare examples that are to be found, the bouquet is dramatic in its power, smelling faintly of lemon. The after-flavours of the wines of these great vineyards will stay in the mouth after the last drop has vanished down the throat.

Wines from the following classified vineyards will be regularly available: Le Montrachet, Bâtard Montrachet, Chevalier Montrachet, Bienvenues Bâtard Montrachet, Les Combettes, Les Pucelles, Les Chalumeux, Les Caillerets (formerly called Les Demoiselles), Les Folatières and Calvoillon. The following growers' labels are widely distributed: Domaine Leflaive, Dupard Aîné, Jean Pascal, Roland Thévenin, Domain Sauzet and Jean Chartron.

The majority of Puligny Montrachet village wines and even single vineyard wines will be found under *négociants'* labels.

Prices are very high, placing them well above the normal level to be afforded in the U.K. for all but special occasion drinking.

CHASSAGNE MONTRACHET

Some additional sorting out of the wine names may be helpful here. Because, on wines lists, the top and most highly priced white Burgundy is Le Montrachet in many instances, then its associates, such as Chevalier, Bâtard and Bienvenue Bâtard, followed by the village wine of Puligny Montrachet, it has been assumed, by inference, that the wines of Chassagne Montrachet are white wines only. This view has only been corrected in recent years by the wider introduction on to merchants' lists of the really excellent red wine from Chassagne Montrachet.

Historically Chassagne Montrachet has always produced more red wine than white. The proportions now are 60 per cent red as against 40 per cent white. Past descriptions of the qualities of red Chassagne drew attention to the fact that the best Chassagne is more similar in character to the wines of the Côte de Nuits than to those of the Côte de Beaune to which it belongs. The reason for this praise lies in the ability of Chassagne to produce dark, fattish wines, with a smoothness which develops with age. For example there is a group of vineyards at the southern end of Chassagne, immediately bordering on Santenay, which are entitled to add 'Morgeot' after the village name. This may also be done with the white wines, where several growers regularly vinify most distinguished qualities of wines. The Domaine Duc de Magenta owns a small plot – the Clos de la Chapelle – which is within the vineyards, L'Abbaye de Morgeot, where the finest wines are produced; the 1976 vintage is a wonder. The village white wines of Chassagne Montrachet can happily be compared with those of Meursault and Puligny during their youth, but some of them lose their refinement when allowed to remain in bottle too long.

Wines from the following classified vineyards will be regularly available: Le Montrachet (white), Bâtard Montrachet (white), Criots Bâtard Montrachet (white), L'Abbaye de Morgeot (red and white), Morgeot (red and white), Le Maltroie (red and white), Les Grandes Ruchottes (white), Les Ruchottes (white), Clos St. Jean (red and white) and Les Bourdriottes (red and white). The following growers' labels are widely distributed: Jean Bachelet, Edmond Delagrange, Domaine Duc de Magenta, Jacques Gagnard Delagrange, Marquis de Laguiche, Albert Morey, Ramonet-Prudhon and Bachelet-Ramonet. Among the *négociants*, Ponnelle, Amance, Audiffred and Drouhin always have a typical and representative village wine.

ST. AUBIN

If, when you reach the RN6 to cross over from the great Montrachet vineyards into Chassagne village, you turn right into the main road, up the hill on the right are two villages, Gamay and St. Aubin. Both produce red and white wines of pleasant, yet never truly great quality, because the vineyards, being on high ground, are exposed to the worst elements of the weather. The red wines are often used for blending into wines labelled Côte de Beaune Villages. The white wines, produced from the more hardy Chardonnay, are really worth trying as the village is now ably promoted by some young growers who are introducing improved methods of viticulture and vinification. It is very rare to see St. Aubin wines offered under vineyard names.

Two growers/*négociants'* labels are widely distributed: Jean Lamy et ses Fils and Roux Père et Fils.

SANTENAY

To me there is a special reason to accord this village more coverage than perhaps its viticultural status deserves. In 1934 Constable's Wine Library published *Burgundy* by Stephen Gwynn. In this book Gwynn acknowledges his intense educational friendship with M. Prosper Maufoux of Santenay, describing him as being very special in his vocation as a *négociant-éleveur*. This term means that M. Maufoux does not grow wines himself but buys from the grower after the vintage and subsequent fermentation, keeping the wines during their time in wood before the bottling. Prosper Maufoux's grandson, Pierre, now directs the family business. He has inherited the same dedication to honesty and integrity – qualities that are precious in Burgundy when dealing with a complex and sometimes tempting commercial prospect.

Prosper Maufoux as a firm have been represented in Great Britain for many years by Deinhard & Company, the famous German wine shippers. When my colleagues and I sought to establish our own direct buying arrangements for the firm of Laytons, we were kindly allowed by Pierre Maufoux to re-establish with him the shipping firm of Marcel Amance et Cie. This name commemorates Marcel Maufoux, who was killed during World War I in the area of Amance in the Argonne, after being decorated for valour on the battlefield. So I am linked in several ways, personal and commercial, with Santenay. For Gwynn, Santenay was his Burgundy 'home', and for me it is my good fortune to follow Gwynn as a visitor and merchant to the Maufoux family. Too many people are cynical about Burgundy wines and, unfortunately, it is easy to taste the evidence of poor wines that hide behind famous *Appellations*. But when you speak with Pierre Maufoux your faith is restored – and it must be said that I am a businessman as well as a lover of good wine, so that I need convincing commercially as well as personally.

Santenay is a large village split into two – Haut Santenay and Bas Santenay – but it is more accurately called Santenay-lès-Bains because the spring, Source Carnot, offers the most lithuated water in Europe, reputedly beneficial for gout and rheumatism. Nearby is a home for retired railwaymen and, close to the village, the Casino de Santenay – a strangely off-beat gambling house, full at weekends of factory workers from Le Creusot but empty during the week. The only building of architectural interest in the village is the Église St. Jean, which has some fine statues from the twelfth and seventeenth centuries.

The road from Chassagne Montrachet will bring you past the major vineyards of Santenay. Here you will notice the very recent replanting of vines further up the hill, on ground formerly left for scrubland when labour became difficult to obtain because of the hard physical work involved on the high sections. These plantations will yield wines of sufficient quality for export in a few years' time.

For the visitor who can spare some minutes for an uphill walk to view the landscape that includes vines, many wild flowers and the two villages of Santenay, I recommend taking the path leading off the main square where the Chassagne road enters the villages out into the vines. (Just ask anyone you meet to point out the path.) On this hill above Santenay there is a fine stone memorial of winged horses sculpted by David Norris placed as a tribute to three of my colleagues killed in the air disaster of March 1974 when an aircraft taking off from Paris crashed, everyone aboard being killed. These three – Nicholas Fripp, Nigel Norcliffe Roberts and Bill Dack – loved Burgundy and knew it well. The memorial is in a magnificent position and the climb will never be regretted.

Santenay is a red wine village, making just a tiny quantity of white wine. It is the last notable village of the Côte de Beaune and the lie of the land alters the direction in which the vines are planted, from facing south-east in Chassagne to due south in Santenay, enabling the vines to get maximum exposure to the sun. Look at the lines in which they are planted and you will see what I mean.

The red wines are a bit of a mixture. They can be found as light and fruity but there are still a few growers with old vines, who produce dark, earthy heavyweights. The former styles tend to be bottled by the growers, the latter to be purchased by *négociants* for the export market, where wines need to stand up to varying storage and climatic conditions and where this heavier style can be synonymous with robustness. Santenay does not produce wines of great stamina, so it is advisable to drink them within six or seven years. The rare white wines are usually very similar to those of Chassagne Montrachet.

Wines from the following classified vineyards will be usually available: Les Gravières, Clos de Tavennes and Le Passe Temps. The following growers/*négociants'* labels are widely distributed: Prosper Maufoux, Marcel Amance, (both the above arrange visits by appointment), Joseph Belland, Ph. Chapelle et Fils-Domaine des Hautes Cornières, Réné Fleurot and G. Prieur.

DÉZIZE-LÈS-MARANGES, CHEILLY-LÈS-MARANGES, SAMPIGNY-LÈS-MARANGES

These three rather broken-down villages are the official end of the Côte de Beaune but are all situated round the hill from Santenay. Although each village has its own *Appellation*, my enquiries indicate that the wines are mostly purchased by *négociants* for their Côte de Beaune Villages blends.

Côte Chalonnaise

The region can best be approached from Chagny, which itself is an easy twenty-minute drive south from Beaune. Chagny has no particular attractions, yet it can be a pleasant stopping place for the night because of the Hôtel Lameloise, which is gastronomically renowned. Other small hotels, both in the town and on the outskirts, are perfectly adequate and modestly priced but the restaurant at Lameloise is special.

If the area is to be explored thoroughly, perhaps by the visitor already familiar with the Côte d'Or, Chalon-sur-Saône would be an interesting base from which to drive out into the Côte Chalonnaise. Chalon-sur-Saône has a busy and varied centre with broad boulevards; the shops are probably better stocked than those in Beaune, although Beaune has sprung into life in the last year or two to cope with the growing affluence of both tourists and the locals. A few minutes at the Musée Denon may be of interest, as here there is equipment and documentation of the pioneer of photography, Joseph Nicephore Niepce (1765–1833). He produced the first primitive photograph – a view from his workroom window at Chalon-sur-Saône – in 1822, and later went into partnership with his better-known countryman Daguerre, whose name is perpetuated by the daguerrotype.

However, for the journey through the vineyards, Chagny

will probably be most visitors' starting point. One should leave the town by the RN481.

The four villages of importance that give their name to the labels line up north to south on the hillsides, facing east in the direction of Chalon-sur-Saône. Despite the renewed interest in this wine region, their names are still pretty well unknown to the wine drinking public.

RULLY

This is the first village on the itinerary. Since 1830 it has been virtually the home of sparkling Burgundy. It was discovered that the white wine from the hillsides, made by combining the grape varieties Aligoté and Chardonnay is perfect for turning into *vin mousseux*, sparkling wine made according to the Champagne method, whereby a secondary fermentation takes place in the bottle. The big shippers took advantage of this and enlarged the trade by sending their own wines to be handled here – these not always being straight Burgundy but sometimes blended wines – so as to provide a specific and maintained style. The owners of land here have increased their production, replanting especially on the highlands above the village, so as to popularise the name Rully, but as far as the white wines are concerned, the Chardonnay grape has to cope with the risks of both hail and frost, very prevalent on this *côte*. The general style of still white Rully is lively and fruity, with a clean, fresh sensation on the palate. The drawback is the shorter life of Rully white, much shorter than the lives of the greater white wines of the Côte de Beaune to the north.

The vineyards of Rully surround the village, creating a compact impression, where the *vignerons* and *négociants* seem happy to spare more time with the visitor than in some of the more fame-affected villages of the Côte d'Or.

MERCUREY

Soon after leaving Rully, you come to Mercurey. The vineyards of Mercurey are widely spread through the surrounding villages of St. Martin-sous-Montaigne and Bourgneuf Val d'Or, which make 95 per cent red wine, with an important annual average production of 125,000 dozen bottles.

About 5 per cent of the production is white, this last being full of character, similar in style to the elegance of Chassagne Montrachet but with the firmness of Meursault. Red Mercurey, as many will know it from export markets, usually has plenty of weight and a definite flavour, including some hint of earthiness and iron. The maturity period is relatively short and there is no need to keep these wines for more than five or six years after their vintage.

Mercurey as a place has no special appeal as a busy road passes directly through the village. Perhaps some of this traffic is caused by the growing number of commercial cellars, owned by shippers using Mercurey as a centre for storing wines in cask. In the region of Mercurey, many vineyards are also owned by shippers, some well known to the export trade, for example, Bouchard Aîné, J. Faiveley, Antonin Rodet and Maurice Prothcau. Off the main road, however, the vineyard lanes are quiet and very pleasant for continuing the wine circuit, with many places that are agreeably secluded for a stop, either to study the map, draw a cork, take a picture, or have a picnic. But do leave the place tidy – tourists have acquired something of an ill reputation for scattering litter.

GIVRY

Givry once enjoyed a reputation for wine alongside that of Beaune and Volnay, its reds being supplied to several royal courts of France and being well known in Paris. After World War I, however, Givry wines fell from favour. In recent years an attempt at revival has been made. The village received its *Appellation Contrôlée* in 1946; before then much of the red wine was sold as Mercurey. Ninety per cent of Givry production is red, the slightly sharp, almost bitter backtaste, which can cut through the richness and finish with a flourish when being drunk with the rich sauces and heavy dishes of Burgundy, can be pleasant and effective. Givry also rounds off early in its life in bottle, so that it may be brought to table without the long-term and expensive maturation some other wines require. Expect from Givry wines a little extra acidity, as in the red wines of the Loire valley.

MONTAGNY

From Givry, the road goes on to Montagny, as a place very much 'old Burgundy', a wine village as it has been for generations, although not particularly picturesque.

The A.O.C. Montagny still means something that I respect. The vineyards produce white only, made from the Chardonnay. Adjacent to Montagny is Buxy, very well known throughout the world of wine because of its excellent Cave Co-operative, where first-rate wines are made and bought by a number of firms whose standards are exacting. Several of the large shippers buy in bulk from the Buxy Co-operative for blending or straight bottling under their own name – a completely legal process. The art of the shipper lies in the blending of wines to create a harmonious result and, of those firms I know who buy from this co-operative, each of their wines is individual, though overall typical of the region. One almost expects to see the names of certain famous establishments on the different vats.

Montagny wines are dry but, with a little time in bottle, can develop a fine, full bouquet and a scale of definite assertive flavours. They need only two or three years to be at their best so don't let them get too old or be beguiled – as so many of the British are – by the unsound belief that an old wine is inevitably better than a young one. This is a foolish generalisation and never more so than when applied to Montagny. The wine of Montagny is the sort of white Burgundy which is still a bargain buy and will give great pleasure. Certain other names, by contrast, not only vary enormously according to the publicity their wines receive but also soar in price if they become fashionable, and in consequence sought after, notably in the U.S.A. Although I regret to say it, the quality of the wines in general may in such circumstances decline.

6

The Food of Burgundy

Some years ago I heard an excited chef/proprietor exclaim *'La gastronomie en France est finie!'* That may be so but you can still eat very well indeed there and nowhere better than in Burgundy. The experience of facing up to the delights of the Burgundian table will, however, be costly unless you have the good fortune to be invited to lunch or to dine with a French family living there. Still, it is of little comfort to others to know that the fine dishes traditional to this area remain alive more strongly in the kitchens of the *vignerons* and *négociants* than in most restaurants, where the menus become increasingly *'touristique'* – aimed at the traveller with more francs than gastronomic sense.

To our generation, obsessed as it is with calories and cholesterol, the culinary history of Burgundy makes staggering reading. Back in the fourteenth century, when the Ducs de Bourgogne ruled over the province from their great palace in Dijon, it was quite normal at a reasonably well-to-do table to sit down to the following dishes:

Soups: Leek soup with bacon; Broth of chicken
First course: Chicken hotpot; Capon
Second course: Frogs' legs fricassee; Snails; Crawfish in aspic
Desserts: Pear compote; Elderberry fritters
Of course this was not peasant fare, but nor was it the menu of a special celebratory occasion!

Today dishes have become a little more refined. The regional specialities most commonly found in the Burgundy restaurants illustrate the immense natural richness and self-sufficiency of the many départements comprising 'La Bourgogne'. A short list of some should start the gastric juices flowing.

Jambon persillé: ham in a jelly flavoured with parsley.
Oeufs en meurette: eggs poached in red wine served on croûtons with a sauce incorporating shallots.
Andouilles: tripe sausages – rather rich.
Jambon de Morvan: raw ham from the Morvan region, a wooded, hilly district immediately west of the Côte d'Or in the direction of the Loire. This is great hunting and shooting country and the ham is first rate. The cure is not particularly strong.
La gougère: a cheese-flavoured pastry puff.
Morilles: many dishes are described as *'aux morilles'*; these are the local field mushrooms, which have a definite though delicate earthy flavour.

Poulet demi-deuil: chicken with the breast threaded with slices of truffle before it is cooked. The black and white colour gives the 'half-mourning' look.

Boeuf à la Bourguignonne: beef, cooked in red wine with onions, mushrooms and cubes of bacon (although French 'bacon' is a more robust form of the meat than anything the Briton may be used to). It is often served accompanied by the wines of the Côte de Nuits, such as Fixin, Morey St. Denis, Gevrey Chambertin or Nuits St. Georges, but I find that the rather flatter-tasting wines of Beaune and Savigny-lès-Beaune are usually more suitable as they seem to absorb and mop up the powerful flavours of the beef stew.

Rable de lièvre: saddle of hare cooked in red wine – a version of 'jugged hare' – and remember, the animal will have fed on the herby upland pastures of the region and its flesh will therefore possess a marked and gamey taste.

Salade à la Bourguignonne: salad made with a curly type of lettuce, with garlic – unless the restaurant suspects that Anglo-Saxon diners eschew the use of the herb – with diced bacon cubes mixed in.

Quenelles de volaille: finely minced or pounded 'sausages' or balls of chicken meat, served with a sauce.

Saucisse en brioche: a worldly version of the sausage roll – a sausage of some type, possibly seasoned with herbs (and remember, the French 'sausage' is higher in meat content than the U.K. banger), in some form of case. When offered *à la vigneronne* it will be accompanied by a red wine sauce. Or it may be presented in a covering of brioche dough, so that it is virtually the size of a small loaf or large roll.

Boudin: the Burgundian version of black pudding – blood sausage.

Haricots au vin rouge: beans cooked in red wine.

Coq au vin: chicken cooked in red wine, usually with a dark-coloured sauce made with the same wine. It is one of the most famous dishes of the region and there are various different recipes. Essentially a peasant dish, it is capable of achieving great gastronomic quality when made by the chef of a good restaurant. *'Coq au Chambertin'* will sometimes appear on menus, but what and whose Chambertin is something I've never seen specified.

Jambon à la lie de vin: a special dish of ham braised in the red wine that has been left over in the cask after the bottling is finished – in other words, the lees of the wine. The deposit endows the dish with great succulence and make a sensational sauce for soaking up with bread, so don't hesitate to 'dunk', as this is a compliment to the cook.

Pouchouse: a stew of freshwater fish from the River Saône, more likely to be featured in small restaurants by the river (or its tributaries) than in towns. Verdun-sur-le-Doubs is well known for *Pouchouse*. The four fish involved are pike, tench, eel and perch, simmered together in a white wine of good quality: Mâcon Lugny, Pouilly Fuissé, Chassagne Montrachet have all been used at various times in the stews served by my friends, who add cream and plenty of garlic cloves, the latter gradually dissolving in the steaming pot during the slow cooking.

Cheese

Burgundians are great cheese eaters but there is no regional cheese of note. As elsewhere in France, expect to be served cheese immediately following the meat course. This is sensible as the cheese then either accompanies the last of the red wine or can herald a fresh bottle if the host's pocket can run to another.

The following cheeses may arrive, sometimes laid on straw or presented in miniature *paniers*, little baskets in the shape of the traditional Burgundian vineyard basket:

Époisses: a soft cheese, rich in flavour, that blends well with the fuller red wines.

Chevrotins: tiny individual goat cheeses, with a hard, dry texture – not specially strong or 'goaty'.

Rigottes: a variety of *Chevrotins*.

St. Florentin: a cow's-milk cheese – rather powerful.

Comté: often served by the wine trade to accompany fine wines and the same style as Gruyère and Emmenthal. It should be fresh and is best in spring and autumn.

Fromage à la crème: a fantastic rich, sweet cream cheese dish. It is served in a mould, to which you add sugar and cream cheese and mix. Of course, you can eat it by itself too.

Where to Eat and How to Drink

The wine villages of the Côte d'Or are a little disappointing as regards eating places, but here are some villages where well-established cafés have given me good traditional dishes, away from the main towns: Gevrey Chambertin, Morey St. Denis, Savigny-lès-Beaune, Montagne de Beaune, Auxey Duresses and Meursault.

By law, French restaurants must display their menus outside and from this menu it is possible to ascertain the price bracket of the establishment. Fixed-price menus are always available, but be careful about any *'Menu touristique'* or *'Menu gastronomique'*, as both will usually be gargantuan and very expensive. When you have sat down and the menu is presented, be sure to go through it; waiters have a habit of opening a menu without indicating the cheapest fixed-price menu on another page and if you're in a hurry, you may not notice this.

The wine list, more often than not, is displayed inside the menu cover and it is never as explicit as its British counterpart: vintages are pencilled in and the names of growers and shippers left out completely. If you want to know these, ask to see the bottles first, making it absolutely clear that they are not to be opened until you say so. Beware of half bottles. The French do not drink them, so stocks are often tired.

My choice of wine when I'm eating out veers away from the expensive anyway, but I hold the view that there is usually a bargain on every list. If you want a white wine, an Aligoté can be clean and refreshingly crisp. For a bargain red, my choice in the past has often wandered into the Côtes du Rhône or Beaujolais districts, but today these have all risen steeply in price. So, unless you want something to assist your study of Burgundy wines or can afford more than 50 francs per bottle, it is frequently sensible to order a simple Bourgogne Rouge or a Passe Tout Grains.

Personally, I avoid 'house' red wines in Burgundy, because the average quality of such wine when sold *en carafe* or *pichet* does not delight my palate; the French certainly prefer drier and more bitter red wines than we British are yet forced to accept, although doubtless this taste will soon be imposed on us. 'Bitterness' may be a harsh description, though I retain the adjective; it may also be fair to say that the French will accept, in their everyday red wines, a higher level of acidity than the public in the U.S. or U.K. will drink.

If you do order a fine old bottle, ask them to decant it. As time may be short, so that the wine may not be able to breathe quickly enough once the cork is removed, it makes sense to decant even if the bottle has no sediment. The waiter may give you the supercilious glare that only a French waiter can achieve, but stick it out and insist. (They always do as you ask in the end.) But, to make up for any bad impression that the wine service may give, you will find the general standard of restaurant service in Burgundy quite outstanding for friendliness and patience with foreign visitors. And it does help if you can manage even a little of the language – it is better to try in French and fail than not to try at all.

Picnics

If you are buying a picnic, remember that items containing a fair amount of fat do tend to be bad travellers. So unless you are going to eat them within a quarter of an hour, or have an insulated bag to keep them cool, don't be tempted into buying a quantity of delicious-looking pâtés, ripe cheeses and portions of made-up dishes that will have become sticky and semi-liquid an hour later if the weather is hot. Don't forget to buy plenty of mineral water from the cold compartment of a shop. This can also be used for washing fruit and salads, which are more refreshing in warm weather at midday than ices and pastries. A wide-mouthed vacuum jar or insulated butter dish will enable you to keep any butter and cheese not used up at once for at least twenty-four hours.

Rather than buying one of the elaborately labelled bottles you may see on supermarket shelves – which may be cheap but possibly not more than an adequate drink – take advantage of being in Burgundy by spending a little more and sampling a local wine. If you buy this from a grower or at a tasting room and wish to cool it, remember that newspaper, soaked in cold water, will keep it fairly cold for at least a short time.

APPENDIX 1

Wine Tasting

by Pamela Vandyke Price

There is nothing difficult about tasting wine, even if some
people suppose it to be a mystery requiring a long initiation
process! The aim of tasting is to discover an enjoyable wine,
either enjoyable to drink immediately or likely to prove
enjoyable after some period of maturation. When you visit a
wine merchant's tasting or attend a tasting party, you are most
likely to be offered samples of wines that are ready or very
nearly ready to drink. When you visit a wine shipper, or
anywhere in the region where wine is produced, you are more
likely to get the chance of trying wines that are as yet not ready
to drink. Indeed, some of the very finest wines do not make
pleasant drinking at all while they are growing up and
developing and there may be little temptation to swallow them.
But although even a very little experience will acquaint you
with different things to look out for in different wines at various
stages in their development, the basic procedure of tasting is the
same.

Wine is a beautiful and interesting commodity – and those
who really know something about it and care for it are delighted
to share their enjoyment and appreciation with even the
humblest beginner as well as with the experienced. So do not be
shy of trying to taste seriously. Ask questions and whenever
possible try to note down your impressions of a wine *while* you
are tasting it – even an hour later, your thoughts will lack
precision. Also, if you remember in detail wines that you like or
do not like your future shopping for wine is greatly helped. No
one wants to risk being a wine bore or wine snob, but the world
of true lovers of wine is wide, hospitable and worthy of
exploration.

Tasting Sense and Tasting Room Manners

The tasting room is the heart of the business of any wine
establishment. Care is taken to ensure that the wines may be
examined as critically as possible, and that nothing should
interfere with this. It sometimes disappoints people to find that
a tasting room is rather a clinical place, usually with a north
light plus very strong artificial lighting, plenty of white on walls
and benches against which the colours of wines may be
examined, and with at least one sink and possibly several
spittoons as well. But the 'picturesque' type of tasting is usually

more in the nature of a party and not for the occasions when large sums of money are being allocated to the buying and selling of a firm's wines.

Visitors to the tasting room will naturally wish to conform to what may be described as 'tasting manners', by not making it difficult for anyone else to make serious use of the room either while they are there, or immediately after their visit. Scent and strongly smelling toilctrics for men as well as for women should ideally be avoided or, if someone has just used scent or been on the receiving end of some pungent preparation at hairdresser or barber, it is worthy mentioning the fact by way of excuse, to show that you are aware this may be a distraction. Don't start to smoke, unless specifically invited to do so, as this may make the tasting room unusable for some while, though if the occasion is not too serious the host may well offer cigarettes in his office, if not actually in the tasting room. Beware of thinking that the shallow metal or enamel cups that often stand about in tasting rooms are ashtrays – they are tasting cups, and should not be casually used!

SHARING GLASSES

At professional tastings, unless someone has a cold, mouth infection or anything that obviously necessitates them keeping a single glass for their own use, it is usual for everyone tasting to do so from a single glass, which will be standing either in front of the bottle from which the tasting sample has been drawn or on a space marked in some way on the tasting bench. Some people are hesitant about sharing a glass, but may be reminded that wine is the second oldest disinfectant in the world. If you are really disinclined to taste from a glass used by anyone else, you should make no bones about asking for one for yourself.

Obviously, a woman does not want to leave lipstick on a wine glass at any time – it looks particularly revolting – and even a slight trace can affect the taste of the wine for anyone coming afterwards in a serious appraisal of wine. But it is a very simple matter to wipe the mouth before tasting, should anyone really be at the stage when they leave traces of lipstick on every eating utensil (quite unnecessary, if lipstick is correctly chosen and applied). Men should be reminded that, if they use strongly smelling soap to wash their hands, or make use of pronouncedly fragrant aftershave lotion or any preparation for hair, they will make the glasses smell just as much as any woman's cosmetic.

A final piece of advice which may seem a little severe though is not so intended: anyone who is trying to form a precise opinion about a wine being tasted requires to be able to give that wine undivided attention. Anyone who, with a false idea of making themselves agreeable, insists on breaking in on the train of thought of the taster at such a moment, peering to see what notes have been written (the experienced taster usually evolves a shorthand which is quite indecipherable to anybody else) and generally making a noise of superficial or frivolous conversation, is likely to be more of a nuisance than a welcome guest in the tasting room. There are plenty of opportunities for asking questions and exchanging points of view without interrupting someone seriously at work, and – in case it should be thought that I am being unnecessarily stern – I must point out that some of the visitors to a tasting room may be those to whom the opportunity is both illuminating and of the greatest importance as regards their future approach to wine. To interfere with an opportunity that may come only rarely, or prevent someone from taking as much advantage as possible out of an experience of serious tasting is both selfish and boorish. The professional may be able to taste on another occasion: the visiting amateur may be deprived of a unique experience by the misplaced bonhomie of someone who really simply wants a drink and would therefore do better to cut short his visit to a tasting room and await the next stage of the proceedings outside.

SPITTING

In an age when virtually any subject can be discussed, it is astonishing that people still display hesitancy and even squeamishness about spitting out samples of wine that they are tasting. A moment's reflection will indicate that to spit out when tasting is the only sensible thing to do: not merely will the mixture of a number of different wines be confusing to the palate and probably upsetting to the stomach, but some samples may be out of condition, others, especially very young wines, undergoing some form of fermentation, so none of them may actually be enjoyable to drink. Spit them out. It is perfectly possible to eject wine from the mouth discreetly and without fuss. If you are tasting samples drawn direct from casks or vats in a cellar, it is usually acceptable to spit on the floor – remember that, if this is stone or cement, there will be some splashback, so try to avoid getting wine on your shoes or those of your companions. In the tasting room, the sink or spittoon will be sluiced down at intervals, even if there is not a tap running to keep everything fresh. Let me reiterate: spit out any samples offered for tasting, unless you are specifically given a portion of wine and advised to drink it. To swallow tasting samples risks giving yourself a stomach upset and will not improve your knowledge or experience of wine.

First Look at the Wine's Appearance

A tasting sample will only occupy a small space in the glass. Its appearance has much to reveal. Ideally, the glass should be perfectly clear and clean and on a stem, though in some regions you may have to make do with small tumblers or possibly a tasting cup of a special type.

The wine should be clear and bright, with something 'living' about it. Do not be concerned that there may be bits (known as 'flyers') in it, as these may be particles from a cask sample, which subsequent filtration may well remove. Their presence, very often, indicates a quality wine, and therefore they are not reasons for condemning the wine in any way.

Tilt the glass away from you at approximately an angle of 45° and hold it against something white, so that you can examine the colour. The living quality should be obvious, rather in the way that the water of a spring is different from the flat dull water drawn from a tap and left to stand for several days. Whether the wine is red or white, it should be pleasant, ideally beautiful to look at and give pleasure to the eye.

What the Wines Indicate by Colour

WHITE WINES

These tend to deepen in colour as they age, and, usually but by no means invariably, the sweeter wines start their life by being more golden than the pale light lemon gold of the drier wines. It is also fairly safe to generalise to the extent of saying that white wines from warm southern vineyards usually start by having a more yellow-straw colour than those from very cold vineyards, which will be pale lemon yellow, or almost very pale green. A really old white wine (old in terms of its maturity, not specifically related to its age in terms of years) may assume almost an orange tinge, reminiscent of some of the dry Madeiras; this, and the sort of smell and taste that can come off such wines result in the term 'maderised' often being applied to them. It does not mean that they are undrinkable by any means, but they will have changed their character.

Look, too, at the actual consistency of the wine in the glass. The way in which it clings to the sides of the glass and trails downwards with the pull of gravity can indicate a wine of great quality if these trails (known as 'legs') are marked. This is also indicative of the glycerine content which will be marked in the wines that naturally contain a certain sweetness.

RED WINES

Red wines tend to grow paler as they age, many of them being purple-red at the outset. It is probably easier for most people to see the different tones of colour in a red wine and it is helpful sometimes to know that, with a very fine wine (whether you like it or not) there tend to be far more distinct tones of colour visible as you tilt the glass than in even a good cheap wine. Look at the 'eye' of the wine at the centre of the liquid, and then see the gradations of colour out to the edge where the wine meets the glass: a young red wine will be purplish down to black, with a rim that may begin to lighten almost to a deep lilac tone. With a little more maturity, it may become reddish and in the end a beautiful crimson-orange with great age. Red Bordeaux probably lightens more throughout its life than red Burgundy, which tends to be very purple at the outset, except in certain years when the colour can be on the light side.

Remember that, with all wines, age is relative. Some wines show signs of great age when they are young in years, simply because they are wines that should be at their peak while comparatively young and fresh; others, including the very greatest red wines and certain whites, remain apparently youthful for many years. Unfortunately, today's economic pressures make it necessary for many wine makers to be able to mature their wines faster than in the past, so as not to tie up their capital; this means that a wine which you may have heard of as taking a long time to mature can be at its peak years before you expected this.

Caution is advisable when appraising wines solely by colour, simply because the control of wine making these days is a very skilled matter and has rightly been judged as important in the appeal a wine makes to its public. If you doubt this, get someone to prepare you two samples of the same red wine, one of them having some additional colouring in it, put there either with culinary colouring matter or by the addition of a few drops of a much darker wine. You will be surprised by the way in which you feel the darker wine to be more 'full-bodied' and possible 'fruity'! Similarly, if you think that colour does not influence taste, try giving a critical appraisal of a wine out of a glass that is a dark definite colour, such as blue, green, or black: you will be astonished to find how, once one sense used in tasting is cut off, all the others are somehow distorted.

Smell the Wine

A wine should have a pleasant healthy smell, which, in certain wines, can be complex but which should always give enjoyment. You will release this and be able to sniff it more easily if you circulate the wine in the glass, holding the glass by the stem or, possibly, by the foot (not as difficult as it looks at the outset) and simply swinging the liquid round, putting your nose into the glass at intervals and sniffing. The aeration of the wine releases the fragrance.

Surprisingly, very few wines actually 'smell of the grape'

although people often wish that they might! A few grapes, notably the Muscat, do possess a distinctive aroma, which is quite often easily identified as 'grapiness', but otherwise, although certain grapes may result in wines smelling of those grapes, the associations with fruit are not always obvious. A wine should smell fresh and clean, but there are certain smells which, with young wines, may be present for a short time, indicating nothing more than that the wine is going through a phase of natural development.

These smells include the slightly beery smell which may mean the wine is still undergoing a stage of fermentation; a vaguely yeasty smell, which sometimes seems present when a wine has recently been bottled; a slightly sharp smell, often described as 'green', which may be present in even the best made wine in a year when the grapes have been unable to ripen perfectly. Or, in some instances, this green smell may mean that the vineyard contains a high proportion of young vines, the use of which is apparent in the early stages of the wine's development. Obviously woody smells can mean that the wine has been matured in new wood, this smell passing with time also, or, if the woodiness is of a soggy sort, it may mean that there is a faulty stave in the cask in which the wine has been matured.

You are unlikely to find 'corked' wine in a sample of a very young wine from the cask, but a complete absence of smell can be slightly sinister in this respect, indicating that something is preventing the wine from giving off its fragrance. It is the 'swimming bath' smell, reminiscent of chlorine, that is for me most definitely associated with corkiness – which, by the way, has nothing whatsoever to do with bits of cork being in the wine. Some people do find that corkiness reminds them of the smell of cork, but I have never been able to see this myself. A musty smell can be indicative of an ill-made wine, but it should not be confused with 'bottle stink'. This is the smell (that is often stale and flat) of the little quantity of air held in the bottle of wine under the cork, which may affect the taste of the first portion poured. A little aeration will cause this to pass very soon.

The good smells, interesting and pleasing to the nose, include a type of fruitiness, the different sorts of which will be associated with the various types of grape when the taster has gained a little experience. Young wines, especially those that are most enjoyable when drunk fairly young when they are at their peak of freshness, usually have an obvious fruity smell. Then there is a crisp almost sharp smell, like the freshness of a good apple, which can indicate the right kind of acidity balancing the fruit. This should be noticed in most young wines, especially those that are dry and light. Wines from cool vineyards tend to have more smell than wines from hot ones. The infinity of delicate, flowery, herby, and subtle depths of scent with which some of the great German and other northern vineyards are associated, and in the reds from vineyards where the vine has to struggle, such as Burgundy and Bordeaux, can be so beautiful, even while the wines are very young that, as is sometimes said, 'it is almost unnecessary to drink when the smell is so fascinating'.

With the finest wines, try to break up the general impression made on you by the smell into the first impact, anything that then reveals itself by further aeration, and finally see whether there appears to be some subtle as yet unrevealed fragrance underneath the other smell. Wines are like people in this respect, the more obvious are not always the most rewarding. Sometimes, right at the end of a tasting, a smell can come out of a wine glass that may indicate something to look forward to in the future. Try to remain alert to register this if it is there.

Taste the Wine

Always adapt tasting techniques to what experience has taught you suits your own abilities best. But the most usual way to taste is to draw a very small quantity of wine – about a tea-spoonful – into the mouth, accompanied by a small amount of air. There is no need to make a loud sucking noise while doing this, but the circumstance of pulling the wine into the mouth, plus some air, seems to sharpen up the impression it can make. Then circulate the wine in your mouth, pulling it over the tongue, letting it run along the sides of the mouth and getting a general 'feel' of what it is like: light/dry/sweetish/thick/thin/assertive/reticent/chewy/attaching itself to the sides of the mouth/attacking the gums (everyone's gums tend to ache after a lot of tasting!). Try to split up the numerous impressions which the wine may have to give you before you spit it out. Don't be hesitant about taking more than one sample in quick succession.

AFTER-TASTE AND FINISH

When you have tasted the wine and have spat out the sample, breathe out sharply – you will be aware of an extra smell, rather than a taste, that passes across the palate. This is the after-taste and it can reveal quite a lot about the wine: for example, it may be far more definitely fragrant than the original bouquet or smell, or it may have a lingering quality, known in wine terms as 'length', both of which can indicate that the wine has great promise and may develop considerably. Or there can be little or no after-taste, when a wine may be described as 'short'.

The way in which the wine leaves the palate is the 'finish'.

Does it finish cleanly, or has it a trace of stickiness? Has it a final flourish of flavour, a definite extra touch of taste, or does it die away rapidly? The finish of any good wine, regardless of price, should be clean, and, with a fine wine, entice the drinker to take more. With a modest type of wine, the finish should at least refresh rather than cloy the palate.

THE WORK OF TASTING

Some people really do not like tasting young wines, and affirm that there is no point in doing so, as they are going to enjoy them when the wines are grown-up. This is quite true, but any musician or artist is fascinated to see someone in the same line of business rehearsing or working. The way in which wines develop is equally fascinating; and, even though no one would claim to know exactly what a wine was going to be like at its peak, any more than even the most experienced human being could judge of the detailed progress of another human's performance, the attempt to relate experience to what a wine is saying at one time or another and the backing of one's own judgement in hazarding a view as to the evolution of a particular wine is one of the most engrossing and challenging exercises. Make no mistake, tasting is hard work. It requires great concentration and results in real exhaustion if you have subjected yourself to a long session. The fact that it is, to a wine lover, perhaps the most exhilarating pursuit of all, is a compensation.

Remember what a particular wine has to give: a wine that should be dry ought not, in general, to lack acidity and be seemingly too sweet. A wine that is meant to develop over a period of years need not always be very amiable or even give very much impression of what it is going to be like when it is in its early stages. A very fine wine usually makes some impression on the taster, though all wines can go through phases when they seem to smell and taste of very little. The medium priced and cheap wines are very difficult to taste: they can risk being very much alike, and experience is necessary to differentiate between their attributes and what may be their deficiencies.

Don't bother yourself with the game most wine lovers play of getting friends to 'taste blind' until you are a little experienced. It is perfectly true that this can be great fun and teach you an enormous amount, as the stark appraisal of a wine about which you know nothing at all can be a great test of your own honesty, courage and relation of the power of your taste memory. The fact that some people, on some occasions, can identify a wide range of wines with complete accuracy, is not, by itself, a tribute to more than the luck of the day and their considerable experience; they can be equally mistaken, with reasons for being so, on other occasions. The beginner can easily be discouraged by making apparently pointless mistakes, so that it is wise not to indulge in this until you have a little general knowledge of wines.

Meanwhile, it is only sense to bear in mind that you are unlikely, for example, to be offered a range of red Bordeaux in the tasting room of a Burgundy shipper or vice versa! Nor, in one wine region, are you likely to be offered a wide range of wines from several other districts. The visitor to Bordeaux who was disappointed in not seeing where 'the sherry wines were made' is not unique! Although a firm may handle a vast range of wines, it is unlikely that the visitor will ever be asked to taste more than one type at a time. What they are offered over a hospitable table, of course, may be very much wider in scope.

Taking Notes

Notes made on the spot are far more valuable than any general impressions recorded even a short time afterwards, but it is extremely difficult to translate taste impressions into words. To put 'good' or 'bad' is really equally useless – how do you know? It may simply be that the wine in question does or does not appeal to you at that stage of your experience. Try, whenever possible, to differentiate between wines that you truly like and wines that you may admire as good but which do not particularly appeal to you. I would recommend any taster to make up his or her own set of tasting terms as far as possible. It is useless making play with technicalities only half understood from books or to use terms which may mean something to one taster but very little to another. With even slight experience, it is possible to translate your own tasting impressions into language that may be generally understood, but if it helps you, for example, to write 'carnations' or 'violets' against a particular type of wine, then do so. You associate this wine with those particular flowers and no one else is obliged to do so. But, if, merely because someone who seems to be authoritative, insists that 'wild thyme' or 'scrubbed oak table' is inevitably associated with a particular wine, do not attempt to agree with them unless you can wholly associate yourself with the experience – it is worthless if you cannot share it, and your own impressions will be more valuable to you if you can make the effort to formulate them in terms that enable you to remember more exactly what you taste.

Always date your tasting notes and be precise about where the tasting was done, if you are not using a tasting sheet provided by the establishment. It is surprisingly easy, especially if the wines are good and seem to become better and better, for the impression at the end of any tasting to be wonderful but confused!

Deterrents to Tasting

There are a few things that make it difficult to taste. Some – smoking, scent, etc. – have been mentioned earlier. Obviously, a cold prevents you from doing so easily, and very few people find it easy to taste after they have had a large midday meal. The morning, when the stomach is fairly empty and both the mind and body are fresh, is probably the ideal time. Otherwise, if you wish to prepare your palate for serious tasting, remember that violently flavoured or piquant foods can make it difficult for you, and this should also be remembered when you are choosing wines to go with a meal. Of course, few people would be silly enough to eat curry, large amounts of pickles, or anything containing a high proportion of vinegar while trying to drink a fine wine, but other things can impair the receptivity of the palate, notably eggs and chocolate. Indeed, a single chocolate make it almost impossible for me to taste for several hours afterwards! Anything very sweet, or a piece of confectionery, will also make it quite impossible to taste for some time – even a medium dry wine will taste incredibly acid after such a thing.

People are sometimes offered crusts of dry bread or biscuits to refresh the palate at a tasting, but there is one thing that you will never accept if you are being serious about the procedure – cheese. Not for nothing do the wine trade say 'we buy on apples, sell on cheese', because the alkalinity of cheese has the effect of making almost any wine taste better than it may perhaps be, whereas the acidity of an apple, or a crisp young carrot, will show up a wine quite brutally – for good or bad.

APPENDIX 2
Glossary of Wine Terms

While most of the major shippers and guided tours will have visits in English, it may be helpful to list some of the expressions that could be met on a cellar visit where only French is spoken. From these adjectives and nouns it should be possible to find a suitable description after tasting a wine or to ask a sensible question during a tour of the cellars when wine making equipment can be seen.

The odd intelligent remark dropped into a conversation or tour will probably prolong the discourse by the enthusiastic response from your host and give you a little breathing space before putting the next French sentence together. To those visitors fortunate enough to have mastered the French language, a fair sprinkling of these words will take the vineyard proprietor or *négociant* into a most serious discussion. Please do not take these words as a definitive list; only the more common words are presented in this guide.

If the situation arises where French is the language of the visit, do remember that it is polite and quite normal to shake hands and state your name – nine times out of ten they will forget it, but don't worry, you have tried.

Tasting

Amer   A bitter taste of excess tannin – can indicate long-living wine.

Austere   Austere – a wine lacking charm.

Bouchonné   A 'corked' wine – the cork has become mouldy and imparts an 'old socks' smell. If this is slight, it will ease when open to the air. If it is heavy, it's undrinkable.

Bouquet   The smell of the wine.

Caractère   The overall impression given by the wine, bearing in mind where it originates.

Cassis   Blackcurrant – occasionally red wine can have a slight overtone of this flavour.

Complet   A well-made wine, with all the necessary constituents of quality.

Corps   Relates to the weight of the flavour in the mouth, too much or too little.

Corsé   A full-bodied wine without necessarily any distinction.

Coupé   Blended.

Dégustation   A tasting – often seen as a sign outside a house or cellar to encourage buyers in to taste. Be prudent – this may mean you will be expected to pay or buy some wine.

Dur   Hard in flavour – more noticeable in young red wines.

Fin   Fine in the sense of being distinguished. Will apply to any wine outstanding in its class.

Finesse   My personal adjective to describe breeding of wine.

Frais   Chilled.

Fruité   Fruity. In both red and white wines, the fruitiness is tasted as a first impression.

Généreux   Big, fat wine, but pleasing; shows its youth and grapiness.

Goût   Taste. Used mostly as part of an expression, for example: *goût de bois* (woody taste); *goût de ferment* (yeasty); *goût de miel* (honey flavour, found in some mature dry white wines); *goût de terroir* ('earthy' – a taste given to some wines by the soil, mostly noticeably in red wines. When excessive, it spoils the balance.)

Maderisé   White wine going brown from age or early oxidation – unpleasant.

Mur   Ripe taste. An excessive fruitiness can indicate a very hot summer and picking conditions during the harvest. The term can apply to red and white wines.

Piqué   Sour.

Plat   Flat, uninteresting in style.

Plein   Full in flavour.

Sec   Dry.

Séché   Dried-out flavour.

Sevère   A harsh, abrasive taste.

Souffre   Sulphur – the standard sterilising agent for wines, casks and vats, and used in white wines to stabilise and prolong life. If overdone the smell comes nastily through – it can tickle the throat and make the taster cough.

Souple   Supple – a wine gently yielding all its flavour.

Tannin   Tannin. An essential organic constituent of wine derived from the roots, stems, pips and grape skins dissolved during fermentation. Noticeable mainly in the red wines, it acts as the fortress of the wine during youth and eases off during maturation. Tastes astringent, dries out the mouth.

Tendre   Tender – applicable to young red wines, the softness of which develops quickly after bottling.

Velouté   Velvety, smooth rich style. Term applied only to red wines.

Vigoureux   An attacking flavour.

Vin de garde   A wine to lay down for several years to mature slowly towards its peak (literally 'a wine to keep').

Vineux   A wine high in alcohol – enough to spoil it.

Wine Making

Acide acetique   Acetic acid, which is always present in wine – in excess it makes the wine taste of vinegar.

Cave   Cellar.

Cep   Individual vine.

Cépage   Any grape variety.

Chaptalisation   A procedure named after Dr Chaptal (who lived in the early nineteenth century). It is permitted in Burgundy to add sucrose (sugar) to the must prior to fermentation if the must is deficient in sugar, so as to increase the final alcoholic content by up to an extra 2°. This practice is still hotly debated but it does permit the grower to improve the balance of his wine.

Climat   Any particular vineyard – i.e. a site.

Clos   An enclosed vineyard, usually surrounded by a wall. If the word is used on a label, the wine must come only from the particular vineyard.

Collage   The fining of the wine, to maintain clarity and remove unwanted particles or bits of skins, etc.

Cru   Growth – describes an individual vineyard of some standing, often classified.

Cuve   A vat, used either for fermentation, blending, or storage.

Depôt   A deposit found in red and white wines after maturing – this sediment is left behind in the bottle when decanting.

Domaine   Vineyard(s) belonging to the same proprietor. *'Mise en* (or *du*) *Domaine'* or *'domaine* Bottled' indicates wine bottled by the proprietor, not necessarily at the vineyard (as is signified by 'château bottling' in Bordeaux and elsewhere) but in the *domaine* cellars. Many *domaines* have vineyards in several villages, centralising their fermentation, storage and bottling activities in just one cellar.

Égrappage   Removal of the grape stalks prior to fermentation.

Fleuraison   Flowering of the vines in the spring.

Grand vin   A term which means nothing at all, but is sometimes seen on a wine list in an attempt to enhance the appeal of a wine.

Haut   High.

Hectare   2.471 acres. Vineyard areas are quoted in hectares (often abbreviated to 'ha').

Lie   Lees or sediment in cask or vat.

Marque (déposée)   Registered trade mark or brand name for standard and basic wines, used by shipper for sales continuity.

Millésime   The vintage date as on the label.

Mise   The bottling.

Moût   The must – crushed grapes and their juices before fermentation.

Nature   Still wine.

Ouillage   Ullage – the process of regular topping up of casks and vats to replace evaporation.

Ouvrée   An old Burgundian vineyard measure of 0.0428 hectare.

Panier à vendange   A straw basket used by grape pickers. A special shape peculiar to Burgundy.

Pasteurisation   A process named after Dr Louis Pasteur (1822–95). The wine is heated to between 54°C and 76°C (130° and 170°F) to destroy all micro-organisms and stabilise the wine.

Pichet   A carafe or jug for wine in restaurants, containing around 50cl.

Pièce   The oak cask used in Burgundy, holding 228 litres (50.2 gallons) (around twenty-four to twenty-five cases of twelve bottles). The equivalent name in Chablis is *'feuillette'*.

Pressoir   The press used for crushing the grapes at vintage time.

Récolte   The harvest.

Réserve   A meaningless term used to dress up the description of a wine by implying superior quality.

Soutirage   The process of racking or drawing off the clear wine into fresh cask or vat, leaving behind the sediment during the period of maturation in wood.

Tastevin   Shallow, irregularly dented tasting cup, usually in silver, with loop and handle for forefinger and thumb. Carried by the wine trade everywhere before glasses were widely available, it is still used in Burgundy, so as to taste in ill-lit cellars, when indentations enable the wine's colour to be clearly seen.

Vin mousseux   A sparkling wine, qualified on the label as being made either by the *'Méthode Champenoise'* or *'Produit en Cuve Close'*. The former applies only to *mousseux* with *Appellation* (as Bourgogne Mousseux A.O.C. *Méthode Champenoise*).

APPENDIX 3
Further Reading

Allen, H. Warner, *Natural Red Wines*, Constable, 1951.

Arlott, John and Fielden, Christopher, *Burgundy – Vines and Wines*, Davis Poynter, 1976. Combines the eloquence of John Arlott and the Burgundy trade background of Christopher Fielden, former export director of Chanson Père et Fils.

Gwynn, Stephen, *Burgundy*, Constable, 1934. Can sometimes be found in second-hand bookshops; one of my favourites but of course out of date.

Gunn, Peter, *Burgundy, Landscape with Figures*, Gollancz, 1976. Essays on the history of the region, interesting to any traveller.

Hanson, Anthony, *Burgundy*, Faber & Faber, 1982. Very personal, entirely frank opinion supported by a wealth of detail.

Johnson, Hugh, *World Atlas of Wine*, Mitchell Beazley, 1971. Ideal geographic study and some help with names of leading growers.

Lichine, Alexis, *The Wines of France*, Cassell, 1956.

Lichine, Alexis, *Encyclopaedia of Wines and Spirits*, Cassell, first edition 1967. Excellent for technical and general information. Some opinions read like facts.

Marrison, L. W. *Wines and Spirits*, Penguin, 1973 (3rd edition).

Michelin, Maps 66 and 70.

Michelin, Green Guide – *Bourgogne*.

Poupon and Forgeot, *The Wines of Burgundy*, Presses Universitaires de Frances, 1974 (revised and updated). The two French masters of Burgundy. Basic details and concise information in an English translation by Edward and Michael Ott.

Shand, P. Morton, *A Book of French Wines*, Penguin, 1964 (revised by Cyril Ray). Originally published in 1928, the information is now out of date, but it makes excellent reading.

Sichel, Allan, *The Penguin Book of Wines*, Penguin, 1965 (revised 1976).

Speaight, Robert, *The Companion Guide to Burgundy*, Collins, 1975. Very good as a historical survey and on places to visit.

Vandyke Price, Pamela, *Enjoying Wine, A Tasting Companion*, Heinemann, 1982.

Waugh, Alec, *In Praise of Wine*, Cassell, 1959.

Yoxall, H. W., *The Wines of Burgundy*, International Wine and Food Society, 1968; Penguin, 1974. Written with great feeling by a true lover of Burgundy.

APPENDIX 4

Appellation d'Origine Contrôlée

The general principle and philosophy of the laws governing the production of Burgundy wines are covered by a system of protection, both for the growers and consumers, that falls within the title *'Appellation d'Origine Contrôlée'*.

There are six main types of controls that have to be scrupulously observed before a wine can claim the relevant 'A.O.C.' These, in brief are:

1.   The delimited geographic area of production. (From this the wine's title will be taken – for example, the *Appellation* 'Beaune' has 540 hectares (1,334 acres) of vineyards allotted a potential A.O.C. if the other conditions are fulfilled.)

2.   The grape varieties permitted to be grown (see pages 26–30) for grapes).

3.   The maximum production of wine that can be made per hectare.

4.   The minimum alcoholic degree of the wine. (Again as an example in the Beaune A.O.C., red wines must reach 10.5° and those of *Premiers Crus* vineyards must reach 11.5° to obtain the A.O.C.)

5.   The treatment to which the wine may be subjected during production and maturing in bulk (in vats or tanks of wood or stainless steel).

6.   The method of cultivation and pruning of the vines.

The A.O.C. Laws

As applicable in Burgundy, these break down into four categories: the generic/regional *Appellation*; the village *Appellation*; the village/vineyard *Appellation*; single vineyard *Appellations*. An explanation of these categories will help to clarify the various labels seen on merchants' lists or in restaurants.

GENERIC AND REGIONAL APPELLATIONS

Bourgogne Grand Ordinaire. This is the lowest A.O.C., dealing with any red, white or rosé wines from the specified area of Burgundy. The grape varieties for red and rosé are: Gamay, Pinot Noir, Tressot and César. For white wines: Chardonnay, Pinot Blanc, Aligoté, Melon de Bourgogne and Sacy.

Production of this quality of wine is no longer important because some of these grape varieties individually gain higher

Appellations as will be seen. Mostly found in local restaurants, Bourgogne Grand Ordinaire is rarely sold with a vintage attached to it, because usually two vintages are blended to attain a pleasant balance and make a wine for quick consumption.

Bourgogne Passe Tout Grains. This is an A.O.C. for both red and rosé wines but it is applied almost exclusively to red wines made from a blend produced from a mixture of grapes in the proportions of two-thirds Gamay and one-third Pinot Noir. It can be pleasant when young and fresh but a few years' bottle age helps the marriage of two wines along and makes it even better.

Bourgogne Aligoté. This concerns only white wines made from the Aligoté grape. In good summers these wines achieve a balance of fruit and acidity and they are ideal for apéritif drinking. Aligoté is the best wine for making a *vin blanc cassis* or *Kir*, (see page 47). Some villages have become well known for their Aligoté's quality – Pernand Vergelesses, Savigny and Bouzeron, also the regions of the Hautes Côtes de Beaune et Nuits.

Bourgogne. This A.O.C. covers red, white and rosé wines. These wines are becoming important in these economically restricted times for the Burgundy drinkers of the British Isles. From this *Appellation* some very decent wines can be purchased, if your merchant can establish their origin – and, of course, if you like them. After all, no matter how grand the name on the label, it is the enjoyment of the wine in the bottle that is the really important thing!

The red wines must come from the classic grape Pinot Noir or they may be made from the Gamay grape if they are produced in the nine senior villages of the Beaujolais region (which is outside the scope of this book). For the white wines only the Chardonnay or Pinot Blanc grapes may be used. The production of red and white Bourgogne A.O.C. can be boosted by some village wines that have either been produced in excess of the permitted limits, or have been found lacking some of the conditions demanded by a village A.O.C. So if a Beaune reaches only 10°, although the village A.O.C. requires 10.5°, it can be declassified to be called Bourgogne. Would you notice the difference? I doubt it, if the wine was sound and well made.

Bourgogne Hautes Côtes de Beaune, Bourgogne Hautes Côtes de Nuits. Both these little-known *Appellations* exemplify the renaissance of wines, beginning in France to fill a certain gap in the range of Burgundy. It is yet to be seen if these A.O.C.s can mean much to wine drinkers outside France. The geographical area of these two *Appellations* is best studied on a map. There is one in the booklet *Beaune – Hautes Côtes et Côtes de*

Beaune, available at l'Office du Tourisme opposite the Hospices de Beaune in the town centre. The vineyards contributing to the two *Appellations* lie on the plateaux and higher ground of their respective *côtes*.

Chablis. This regional *Appellation* is discussed in full on pages 68–73.

VILLAGE APPELLATIONS

In the table at the end of this section the various Burgundy *Appellations* are broken down by category so as to show at a glance the standing and distribution of any wine name or label that you may see. Village *Appellations* are precisely as described – that is, the wine name on the A.O.C. label will come from the specific vineyard to which the nearby village has given its name. From these lists all the world-famous Burgundy wine names can be traced.

The original delineation of these village *Appellations* must have caused joy, resentment and sometimes cynical apathy, according to who owned what. Ancient village and parish boundaries were ignored; attention to the lie of the land, known wine qualities and historical reference were the deciding factors for the I.N.A.O. (Institut National des Appellations d'Origine – the body which determines the A.O.C.s). Even so some minor anachronisms remain. For example, Santenots is a fine red wine vineyard nominally in Volnay but actually largely in Meursault, yet the whole production (within the A.O.C. limits) is entitled to be called Volnay Santenots (not Meursault Santenots). As another example, but of slighter importance, the dividing line between the A.O.C. limit of Puligny Montrachet and Chassagne Montrachet goes straight through the middle of the greatest vineyards, both Le Montrachet and Bâtard Montrachet!

These village divisions also create, simply by force of nature, varying sizes of areas with *Appellations*, so that Beaune has a 'surface' area of vines of 540 hectares (1,334 acres), with an average crop of 9,300 hectolitres. Pommard, its neighbour, has a 'surface' area of vines of 340 hectares (840 acres), yet produces an average 10,500 hectolitres. Going down to the smaller villages, tiny Monthélie, next up from Volnay, has only 93 hectares (229 acres) of vines, producing 2,050 hectolitres. So it will be appreciated that one A.O.C. may be well known simply because its area is such that a lot of wine can be made – or vice versa.

At this village level of *Appellation Contrôlée*, one may see a grower's label or a *négociant*'s label, which brings us to another point. Growers' labels for a village *Appellation* do not necessarily indicate that the wine comes from one single vineyard. This is because growers may own several plots in the same village and from these they may blend the wines for the village A.O.C. Of course the style of vinification is the same and in some cases all their grapes will ferment together; in others they keep the different lots separate to blend later, during the wine's maturation in wood. *Négociants'* village wines will usually be a blend of wines from various growers.

Côte de Beaune Villages. This *Appellation* is quite different from that of Côte de Beaune. It is used for red wines only, which must attain a minimum degree of 10.5° and come from sixteen *Appellations* of the Côte de Beaune. For this A.O.C. the wine must be a blend of two *Appellations* or more from the following: Dézize-lès-Maranges, Cheilly-lès-Maranges, Chassagne Montrachet, Puligny Montrachet, Meursault, Auxey Duresses, Chorey, St. Aubin, Santenay, Meursault Blagny, Monthélie, Savigny-lès-Beaune, Ladoix, Pernand Vergelesses. Obviously the blending is the total arbiter of the eventual style. Perhaps the general characteristics of such wines are a robust, generous flavour, needing three or four years' bottle age to show at their best.

Côte de Beaune. Now rarely seen, this *Appellation* covers small parcels of vineyards above Beaune on the Montagne de Beaune. Do not confuse it with Côte de Beaune Villages.

Côte de Nuits Villages. Five villages combine to make up this *Appellation* but only one, Fixin, has its own village *Appellation*. The villages are: Fixin, Brochon, Prissy, Comblanchien and Corgoloin. The *Appellation* is mainly for red wine, which must reach 10.5°. This *Appellation* was formerly called 'Vins Fins de la Côte de Nuits'.

Crémant de Bourgogne, Bourgogne Mousseux. These A.O.C.s are really old wines under new names. Bourgogne Mousseux was thought to be a non-commercial title for a sparkling wine, so in 1975 the *Appellation* Crémant de Bourgogne was created. The basic requirements are that the wine must be made by the *'Méthode Champenoise'* (the Champagne method) and be *Appellation* Bourgogne Blanc. Of this, 30 per cent must come from the noble grape variety Chardonnay; otherwise the Aligoté is used because of its suitable acidity, which is a requisite for quality sparkling wines. If a stand-in for Champagne is needed, then the sparkling wines of Burgundy can be the next best thing, but be careful – many sparkling wines are in fact made in the Burgundy region from wines brought in from other districts; the wines do not have a Burgundy *Appellation*, yet the shipper's name and address will give the impression that they are sparkling Burgundy – until you study the label.

VILLAGE/VINEYARD APPELLATIONS

There is no classification of Burgundy vineyards with the same historic and commercial significance as the 1855 Paris Exhibition classification of the wines of the Gironde (Bordeaux). However, several authoritative attempts have been made to distinguish the various grades of quality from the Côte d'Or vineyards.

Basically, there are three classes of vineyards: *Grand Cru* (Great growth); *Premier Cru* (First growth) and *Deuxième Cru* (Second growth). There have been classifications down to Third growths but today these have mostly disappeared. It is the first- and second-growth wines that are the subject of this section.

Premier Cru and Deuxième Cru. In the case of *Premier Cru* (First growth) vineyards, the name of the village, plus the vineyard name, must appear on the label in the same size of lettering. For example: Beaune Bressandes, giving the village (here a town) name Beaune, plus the vineyard Bressandes. The words *'Premier Cru'* or *'1er Cru'* may also appear if wished by the source of supply.

The name of the wine will be followed on the label by the words *'Appellation Contrôlée'* or, again, if wished 'Appellation Beaune Bressandes Contrôlée', or even 'Appellation Beaune 1er Cru Contrôlée'. If a grower or *négociant* blends two *Premier Cru* vineyards together from the same village, he loses the right to the vineyards' specific names as far as the A.O.C. is concerned, but he is permitted to state on the label 'Beaune 1er Cru', for example.

For *Deuxième Cru* vineyards, the name of the village must appear in lettering twice the size of the vineyard name. For example: 'Beaune Belissand, Appellation Beaune Contrôlée', the word 'Beaune' being twice the size of the word 'Belissand'. In practice, very few *Deuxième Cru* vineyards are now offered under the vineyard name, as the village name is sufficient for the market and the retail customer.

SINGLE VINEYARD APPELLATIONS

Here we arrive at the top of the vine. The *Grands Crus* are the most excellent and highly prized vineyards in the world and, because of their distinction, these vineyards are entitled – within production limits – to announce their names on the bottle without making reference to their specific village. For example: 'Bonnes Mares, Appellation Bonnes Mares Contrôlée'. The Bonnes Mares vineyard actually extends over the boundary between the village A.O.C.s of Chambolle Musigny and Morey St. Denis in the Côte de Nuits, but the vineyard – Bonnes Mares – is the important name, surpassing the names of Chambolle Musigny and Morey St. Denis.

Among the white wines, the vineyard Le Montrachet is in the Côte de Beaune, actually half of it in Chassagne and half in Puligny – but no matter; neither village need be acknowledged on the label. It's the 'Le Montrachet' vineyard that's the great wine.

In some instances, the *Grand Cru* name has been craftily attached to the village name so as to add lustre to the latter and with maybe an eye to attracting sales. Hence 'Chambolle Musigny', where the village of Chambolle added that of Musigny, its most renowned vineyard, to its own. Nuits took St. Georges to itself in 1892, but alas, the famous St. Georges vineyard of Les St. Georges was not nominated by the I.N.A.O. in the 1937 classification as one of the thirty-one *Grands Crus*. To get this wine you have to look for a label that specifies 'Nuits St. Georges Les St. Georges'.

If the opportunity ever presents itself to you to taste or consume a bottle of *Grand Cru* Burgundy, as with all fine wine, do not rush the experience. These wines have a lot to say for themselves and will not be hurried. They deserve calm, leisurely appraisal.

DECLASSIFIED WINES

More specialist information relating to the laws of A.O.C. will be found in the chapter dealing with the way in which Burgundy is made (pages 27–49). However, there is one word often heard and read – 'declassification' – that can be a mystery unless the production limits are understood in relation to the A.O.C.

With the increase of technical assistance available to the *vigneron*, the average quantities produced in the Côte d'Or began to rise. Burgundy sales improved, but the laws of A.O.C. allowed most Côte d'Or villages only a top limit of 35 hectolitres of wine per hectare; yet this increased know-how resulted in some considerable excesses above the permitted quantities for perfectly good reasons. Up until 1974 the A.O.C. laws allowed the growers to declassify these extra quantities downwards, to lower *Appellations*. Thus a grower in Pommard who made 40 hectolitres of wine from 1 hectare of vines would be allowed to declassify 5 hectolitres of this to the A.O.C. Bourgogne Rouge. In really abundant years such as in 1973 the A.O.C. authorities did permit certain increases of *rendement* and the 35-hecto limit was increased to 45. These production limits had not been satisfactory from many points of view for some years and by 1974 new legislation was ready for enactment and a new system of production control was introduced.

In future the A.O.C. authorities will, after consultation,

announce the annual permitted levels per hectare immediately following the harvest. Each grower will be granted an extra 20 per cent over this top figure but, in order to gain the full *Appellation*, he must submit his wine for official approval within a short time of the vintage. But there is a snag: if his sample is not then considered suitable, he loses the *Appellation* for the whole of his crop. I should not like to be present when a grower hears of this latter fate! For, obviously, a wine only permitted to bear an A.O.C. lower in the *Appellation* scale is unlikely to fetch the price of an A.O.C. that is graded higher, however good the wine itself may be. There are certain more complicated aspects of this quantity control that will be without interest for the reader. The description as I have given it brings out the basic concept: the new regulations do allow higher levels of wine production but also, for the first time, some true quality control is exerted.

These laws of protection and encouragement are not perfect but without them the wine trade would be a nasty free-for-all and muddle. My very minor criticism overall is that the A.O.C. establishes a social order of vineyards and, thereby, a price above the real tasting value of the wine; this price is kept up by a world demand, lacking in information about the true relative merits that can change rapidly over a short succession of vintages. All this is yet another reason why you should drink the wine and not the label – however famous the name on it may be.

Burgundy A.O.C.s

Aloxe Corton	Village
Auxey Duresses	Village
Bâtard Montrachet	Vineyard
Beaune	Village
Bienvenues Bâtard Montrachet	Vineyard
Blagny	Village
Bonnes Mares	Vineyard
Bourgogne Aligoté	Generic/regional
Bourgogne Blanc	Generic/regional
Bourgogne Hautes Côtes de Beaune	Generic/regional
Bourgogne Marsannay La Côte	Rosé – Village
Bourgogne Passe Tout Grains	Generic
Bourgogne Rouge	Generic/regional
Chablis	Regional
Chambertin	Vineyard
Chambertin Musigny	Village
Chapelle Chambertin	Vineyard
Chassagne Montrachet	Village
Cheilly-lès-Maranges	Village

Chevalier Montrachet	Vineyard
Chorey-lès-Beaune	Village
Clos de la Roche	Vineyard
Clos de Tart	Vineyard
Clos de Vougeot	Vineyard
Clos St. Denis	Vineyard
Corton	Vineyard
Corton Charlemagne	Vineyard
Côte de Beaune	Generic/regional
Côte de Beaune Villages	Generic/regional
Côte de Nuits Villages	Generic/regional
Crémant de Bourgogne	Generic/regional
Criots Bâtard Montrachet	Vineyard
Dézize-lès-Maranges	Village
Echézeaux	Vineyard
Fixin	Village
Gevrey Chambertin	Village
Givry	Village
Grands Echézeaux	Vineyard
Griotte Chambertin	Vineyard
Ladoix	Village
Latricières Chambertin	Vineyard
Mazis Chambertin	Vineyard
Mazoyères Chambertin	Vineyard
Mercurey	Village
Meursault	Village
Montagny	Village
Monthélie	Village
Montrachet	Vineyard
Morey St. Denis	Village
Musigny	Vineyard
Nuits St. Georges	Village
Pernand Vergelesses	Village
Petit Chablis	Generic/regional
Pommard	Village
Puligny Montrachet	Village
Richebourg	Vineyard
Romanée	Vineyard
Romanée Conti	Vineyard
Romanée St. Vivant	Vineyard
Ruchottes Chambertin	Vineyard
Rully	Village
St. Aubin	Village
St. Romain	Village
Sampigny-lès-Maranges	Village
Santenay	Village
Savigny-lès-Beaune	Village

Tâche, La	Vineyard
Volnay	Village
Volnay Santenots	Vineyard
Vosne Romanée	Village
Vougeot	Village

Index

after-taste 124
agents 12–13
Aligoté grape 20, 26, 29–30, 71, 73, 89, 90, 110, 116, 133, 136
Aloxe Corton 65, 66, 88, 89, 90, 91, 101, 139
Amance, Marcel, et Cie 53, 59, 89, 106, 107, 109
André Frères 88
Angeville, Marquis d' 45, 100
Appellation d'Origine Contrôlée (A.O.C.) 8, 133–41
Armancon Valley 74
Armand, Comte 99
assemblage 12
Arnoux Père et Fils 91
Audiffred 106
Autun 102
Auxerre 68, 72, 74
Auxey Duresses 65, 97, 100–1, 102, 115, 136, 139
Aux Guettes 90
Aux Vergelesses 90
Avallon 67, 68, 73

Bachelet, Jean 106
Bachelet-Ramonet 106
Bâtard Montrachet 104, 105, 106, 135, 139
Beaujolais 1, 2, 22, 26, 29, 83, 102, 116, 134
Beaune 1, 3, 8, 12, 16, 22, 46, 52, 53, 54, 56, 62, 65, 66, 69, 76, 80, 82, 88, 89, 90, 91–7, 109, 111, 114, 135, 139, *see also* Hospices de Beaune
Beaunois grape 70
Beauroy 71
Beine 68, 72
Bélin 49, 76
Belland, Joseph 109
Bertu 72
Bienvenues Bâtard Montrachet 105, 106, 139
Billardet-Gonnet 99
Blagny 102, 103, 104, 136, 139
blanc de blancs 48
Blanchots 70

Boillot, Henri 100
Bois de Corton 30, 65, 88, 89
Boisset, J. C. 76
Bonneau du Mattray 89
Bonnes Mares 52, 83, 137, 139
Bordeaux 6, 16, 50, 54, 55, 56, 61, 126, 137
bottle shapes and sizes 50–1
'bottle stink' 123
bottling 8–11, 42–3
Bouchard Aîné 111
Bouchard Père et Fils 12, 49, 53, 57, 83, 92, 93, 100
Boulanger, Ch. Genot 104
Bourée, Pierre 85, 86
Bourgneuf Val d'Or 110
Bourgogne 134
Bourgogne Aligoté 29, 30, 48, 71, 73, 134, 139
Bourgogne Blanc 48, 51, 139
Bourgogne Grand Ordinaire 71, 73, 133–4
Bourgogne Hautes Côtes de Beaune 134, 139
Bourgogne Hautes Côtes de Nuits 134
Bourgogne Marsannay La Côte 139
Bourgogne Mousseux 48, 136
Bourgogne Passe Tout Grains 26, 29, 116, 134, 139
Bourgogne Rouge 10, 48, 51, 82, 116, 139
Bourgros 70
Bouze-lès-Beaune 65, 91
Bouzeron 134
brandies 24, 94
Brochon 75, 86, 136
Buxy 66, 101, 111
buying Burgundy 56–9
Caillerets 99
Calvoillon 105
Camus 86
Cassis liqueur 30, 47
Cazetiers 85
Cellier Volnaysien 100
César grape 133
Chablis 1, 2, 26, 28, 30, 62, 65, 67–74, 135, 139

Chagny 21, 66, 98, 109
Chalon-sur-Saône 5, 109, 110
Chambertin 84, 85, 139
Chambertin Clos de Bèze 84, 85
Chambolle Musigny 1, 51, 52, 65, 81, 82–3, 137, 138, 139
Champ Canet 105
Champagne 2, 27, 48, 136
Champans 99
Champy Père et Fils 80
Chanson Père et Fils 12, 57, 83, 89, 90, 93, 102
Chapelle Chambertin 84, 139
chaptalisation 38–9, 45, 130
Chardonnay grape 9, 26, 28–9, 35, 48, 70, 72, 89, 101, 107, 110, 111, 133, 134, 136
Charlemagne, Emperor 14
Charles le Téméraire, Duke of Burgundy 15
Charmes Chambertin 84
Chartron, Jean 105
Chassagne Montrachet 1, 28, 29, 35, 45, 47, 65, 80, 97, 102, 105, 106, 108, 109, 110, 115, 135, 136, 139
Châteaux
  de Chorey 91
  de Corton 88
  de Meursault 104
  de Monthélie 100
  de Pommard 98, 99
Châtillon-sur-Seine 14
Chauvenet, F. 48, 76
cheeses of Burgundy 115
Cheilly-lès-Maranges 109, 136, 139
Chemilly 72
Chenôve 3, 87
Chevalier Montrachet 104, 105, 106, 140
Chevalières 104
Chevaliers du Tastevin 17–19, 22–3, 81
Chevaliers des Trois Ceps 20
Chevrets 100
Chitry 20
Chorey-lès-Beaune 45, 88, 91, 136, 140

Cistercians 6, 15, 79, 81
Cîteaux 15
Clair Daü 87
Clairvaux 15, 21
claret 47, 60
Clerget 99
climate 6
Clos des Angles 99
Clos de la Bussière 83

Clos de la Chapelle 106
Clos du Chapitre, Chenôve 87
Clos du Chapitre, Fixin 86
Clos des Chênes 51, 99–100
Clos de la Commaraine 98
Clos des Corvées 76
Clos de la Garenne 105
Clos de la Justice 85
Clos des Lambrays 83
Clos de la Maréchale 76
Clos Micot 98
Clos du Moulin des Moines 101
Clos Napoléon 87
Clos de la Perrière, Fixin 86
Clos de la Perrière, Vougeot 81
Clos du Prieuré 81
Clos de la Roche 83, 140
Clos du Roi, Chenôve 87
Clos du Roi, Corton 89
Clos St. Denis 83, 140
Clos St. Jean 106
Clos de Tart 15, 83, 140
Clos de Tavennes 109
Clos de Vougeot 6, 15, 17, 18, 19, 22–3, 78–81, 140
Cluny 15, 66, 102
collage 41
Combe de Lavaux 85
Comblanchien 3, 74, 75, 136
Comité de Bourgogne 21
commissionaire en vins 11
Corgoloin 3, 74, 75, 136
'corked' wine 123
corks 56
Corney and Barrow 52
Corton 1, 14, 29, 45, 54, 87–91, 93, 96, 140
Corton Charlemagne 14, 46, 47, 65, 88, 89, 90, 95, 140
Côte de Beaune 1, 2, 3, 4, 5, 21, 25, 26, 29, 44, 65, 88, 90, 91–109, 136, 138, 140
Côte de Beaune Villages 91, 92, 107, 109, 136, 140
Côte de Blancs 102–4
Côte Chalonnaise 1, 3, 5–6, 26, 29, 30, 48, 101, 109–12
Côte de Dijon 3
Côte de Lechet 71
Côte de Nuits 1, 2, 3–5, 26, 29, 44, 65, 74–87, 88, 92, 94, 106, 114, 137
Côte de Nuits Villages 75, 86, 136, 140
Côte d'Or 1, 2–3, 5, 6, 8, 14, 19, 26, 29, 30, 31, 34, 38, 40, 54, 55, 69, 73, 74, 75, 87, 89, 93, 99, 109, 110, 115, 137, 138

Côtes du Rhône 116
Coulanges-la-Vineuse 73
coulure 35
courtier de campagne 11
Cousin, River 73
Cousinerie de Bourgogne 19–20
Cras 81
Crémant de Bourgogne 136, 140
Criots Bâtard Montrachet 105, 106, 140
Cruse 76
Cure, River 73
Cusset 76
Cuvée Boillot 101
Cuverie des Ducs de Bourgogne 87

decanting 59–61
declassified wines 138–9
Deinhard and Company 107
Delagrange, Bernard 100
Delagrange, Edmond 106
Delagrange, J. G. 106
Deuxième Cru 137
Dézize-lès-Maranges 5, 109, 136, 140
Dijon 1, 3, 14, 16, 21, 22, 47, 48, 65, 66, 87
Domaine Bertagna 81
Domaine Charles Noëllat 78
Domaine Comte Lafond 104
Domaine Duc de Magenta 106
Domaine Dujac 83–4
Domaine Gagnard Delagrange 45, 106
Domaine Gros 78
Domaine Henri Lamarche 78
Domaine Jacques Prieur 104
Domaine Leflaive 105
Domaine Parent 54
Domaine de la Pousse d'Or 100
Domaine du Prieuré 81
Domaine de la Romanée Conti 77, 78, 101, 140
Domaine St. Michel 34
Domaine Sauzet 105
Domaine Tollot Beaut 45
Domaine Varoilles 86
domaines 7–8, 54, 130
'downy mildew' 35
Drouhin, Joseph 12, 57, 86, 93, 106
Drouhin, Robert 46
Drouhin-Laroze 86
Dubreuil Père et Fils 89
Dupard Aîné 105

échantillon 51
élevage 10
Engel, René 78

Exposition Générale des Vins de Bourgogne 21

Faiveley 17, 53, 76, 80, 86, 111
fermentation 39–42, 43
Fête de la Vigne et du Vin 21
Fielden, Christopher 83
Fine Bourgogne 49
fining 41
'finish' 124–5
Fixin 3, 65, 75, 86, 101, 114, 136, 140
fleuraison 36
Fleurot, Réné 109
Foire Gastronomique 22
Foire Nationale des Vins 21
Foire aux Vins de table 21
food of Burgundy 113–17
Fourchaume 71
Fremiets 100
frost 31, 34

Gamay 29, 107
Gamay grape 26, 29, 133, 134
Geisweiler 48
Geisweiler Domaine Gouges 76
Germain, J. 91
Germain, J. A. 104
Gevrey Chambertin 1, 65, 83, 84–6, 114, 115, 140
Givry 1, 5, 111, 140
Goutte d'Or 104
Grand Cru 70, 137–8
Grants of St. James 52
grape varieties 26–30, 133
Grenouilles 70, 71
Griotte Chambertin 84, 140
Grivelet 76
growers 53–4

hail 35
Hardy, Stephen 15
Hospice de Nuits St. George 75–6
Hospices de Beaune 16, 20, 21, 22, 24, 49, 66, 75, 76, 93–7, 101, 102

Île de Vergelesses 89
Irancy 20, 67, 73

Jaboulet-Vercherre 12, 51, 80, 88, 98, 99
Jadot, Louis 57
Javillier, Raymond 104
Jean Sans Peur, Duke of Burgundy 15
Joigny 67, 68
Julius Caesar 14

Kir, Canon Félix 48
Kir 30, 47–8, 134

L'Abbaye de Morgeot 106
labels 51–6
Labouré-Roi 76
La Combe aux Moines 85
Ladoux (Serrigny) 5, 90, 136, 140
La Dominode 90
Laguiche, Marquis du 106
La Mazière 87
Lamy, Jean, et ses Fils 107
La Petite Chapelle 85
Laplanche, M. 98
La Reine Pédauque 80
La Romanée 77, 140
La Tâche 77, 141
Latour, Louis 12, 46, 49, 53, 57, 88, 89
Latricières Chambertin 84, 140
Laytons 52, 107
Le Corton 88, 89
Lejay Legoute 47
Le Maltroie 106
Le Montrachet 104, 105, 106, 135, 138
Le Musigny 51, 81, 82
Le Passe Temps 109
Leroy, J. 101
Les Amoureuses 61, 82
Les Arvelets 98
Les Baraques 85
Les Bienvenues 104, 105
Les Bourdriottes 106
Les Bressandes 89, 137
Les Caillerets 105
Les Chalumeux 105
Les Champeaux 85
Les Champs Fuilliot 100
Les Charmes, Chambolle Musigny 82
Les Charmes, Meursault 104
Les Clos 70, 71
Les Combettes 105
Les Duresses 101
Les Echézeaux 78, 140
Les Épenots 98
Les Fichots 89
Les Folatières 105
Les Fourneaux 71
Les Genevrières 104
Les Grandes Ruchottes 106
Les Grands Echézeaux 78, 140
Les Gravières 109
Les Hervelets 87
Les Lavières 90
Les Marechaudes 89

Les Perdrix 76
Les Perrières 104
Les Pézerolles 98
Les Porrets 76
Les Procès 76
Les Pruliers 76
Les Pucelles 105
Les Referts 105
Les Ruchottes 106
Les Rugiens 98
Les St. Georges 76, 138
Les Sorbets 83
Les Vaucrains 76
Liger-Belair 76, 77
Lignorelles 72
Ligny le Chapel 68
Lupé-Cholet 76

Mâcon 21, 83
Mâcon Lugny 115
Mâconnais 1, 29, 83, 102
Maligny 72
malo-lactic fermentation 10, 41, 43
marc 24, 40, 48–9, 94
Marc de Bourgogne 48–9
Marconnets 90
Marey-lès-Fussey 29
Marion, Dr. 87
Marsannay 65, 87
maturation 40–2, 46, 59
Maufoux, Marcel 107
Maufoux, Pierre 59, 107, 108
Maufoux, Prosper 45, 53, 107, 109
Mazis Chambertin 84, 94, 97, 140
Mazoyères Chambertin 84, 140
Melinots 71
Melon de Bourgogne grape 133
Mercurey 1, 5, 29, 66, 110–11, 140
Mérode, Prince de 89
méthode ancienne 40
méthode Champenoise 48, 110, 136
Meursault 1, 11, 24, 25, 28, 46, 47, 65, 94, 96, 97, 99, 100, 101, 102–4, 105, 106, 110, 115, 135, 136, 140
micro-climates 6
mildew 35
millerandage 35
Moillard 76
Mommessin family 15, 83
Monnier, Réné 104
Montagne de Beaune 65, 91, 115, 136
Montagny 1, 5, 66, 111–12, 140
Montée de Tonnerre 71
Monthélie 54, 65, 97, 100, 101, 135, 136, 140

Montmains 71
Montrachet 28, 140
Monts de Milieu 71
Morey, Albert 106
Morey St. Denis 1, 15, 65, 81,
    83–4, 114, 115, 137, 138, 140
Morgeot 106
Morin Père et Fils 80
Musigny 138, 140

Napa Valley, California 29
Napoleon I, Emperor 16
négociants 9, 11, 12, 42, 53, 59
Notre Dame du Tart 15
Nuits St. Georges 1, 2, 3, 8, 30, 48,
    51, 52, 53, 65, 69, 74–6, 80,
    114, 138, 140

oak casks 8, 9, 40
oïdium 35
ouillage 41

Pascal, Jean 105
Pasteur, Louis 39
Patriache Père et Fils 104
'Paulée, La' 25, 103
Pernand Vergelesses 29, 74, 88, 89,
    91, 96, 134, 136, 140
Perret, Denis 57
Petit Chablis 72–3, 140
Philippe le Bon, Duke of Burgundy
    15, 16
Philippe le Hardi, Duke of Burgundy
    15
phylloxera 3, 72, 86
picnics 116–17
Piliers Chablisiens 20
Pinot Blanc grape 133, 134
Pinot Noir grape 9, 20, 26–7, 28,
    29, 35, 38, 87, 101, 133, 134
Pommard 1, 8, 10, 54, 65, 91, 93,
    97–9, 100, 135, 138, 140
Ponnelle, Pierre 80, 81, 86, 106
Poruzots 104
Pouilly Blanc Fumé 73
Pouilly Fuissé 28, 115
Pousse d'Or 100
Prémeaux 74, 75, 76
Premier Cru 55, 71, 137
pressing 39
Preuses 70
Prieur, G. 109
Prissey 75, 136
Protheau, Maurice 111
Prunier, Michel 101
pruning 31, 34
Puligny Montrachet 1, 44, 46, 47,
    65, 97, 101, 102, 103, 104–6,
    135, 136, 140

racking 41
Ramonet-Prudhon 106
Rapet Père et Fils 89
Rhône, River 1, 7, 50
Richebourg 78, 140
Rodet, Antonin 111
Rodier, Camille 17
Romanée Conti 77, 140
Romanée St. Vivant 77, 140
Ropiteau Frères 104
Roumier 81, 83
Rousseau, Armand 86
Roux Père et Fils 107
Ruchottes Chambertin 84, 140
Rully, 1, 5, 48, 66, 110, 140
Runciman, Sir Stephen 15

Sacy grape 71, 73, 133
St. Aubin 107, 136, 140
St. Benigne Abbey 14
St. Bernard 15
St. Bris 20
St. Bris-le-Vineux 73
St. Cassien 19, 20
St. Jacques 85
St. Martin-sou-Montaigne 110
St. Romain 97, 100, 101–2, 140
St. Vincent 19, 20
Sampigny-lès-Maranges 109, 140
Sancerre 73
Santenay 1, 5, 34, 45, 53, 59, 65,
    89, 97, 102, 107–9, 136, 140
Santenots 99, 100, 135
Saône-et-Loire 1, 21
Saône, River 5, 7, 74, 114
Sauvignon grape 73
Savigny-lès-Beaunne 19, 20, 29, 53,
    89–90, 91, 96, 114, 115, 134,
    136, 140
Serein, River 70, 71
Seysses, Jacques 83
shippers 7, 9, 11–13, 52–3, 59
Sichel, H. and Sons 52
smell of wine 122–4
soil 4, 5, 6–7
Solutré 14
soutirage 41
sparkling Burgundy 20, 48, 110, 136
Suremain, R. and B. de 100

taille Guyot 31, 34
tastevin 131
tasting 118–27
Thévenin, Roland 101, 102, 105
Thomas, Wynford Vaughan 16
Toisin d'Or 16
Tollot Beaut 45, 89

Tonnerre 67, 68, 72, 74
Tournus 60, 66
Tressot grape 133
Trois Ceps, Confrèrie des 20
Trois Glorieuses, Les 22–5, 60, 94, 102

Vaillons 71
Valmur 70
Varoilles 85
Vaucoupin 71
Vaudésir 70
Védrenne 47
véraison 35
Verdun-sur-le-Doubs 115
Victoria Wine 52
Vienot, Charles 76
Vigne de l'Enfant Jésu 92
village *appellations* 135–7
Villamont, Henri de 53
vin blanc cassis 30, 47–8, 134
vin mousseux 48, 110, 131

vineyard *appellations* 137–8
vineyard calendar, cycle 30–6
Vinothèque, Beaune 57
vins de garde 46
vintage time 32, 36–8
vintages 43–7
Voarick, R. 91
Voguë, Comte Georges de 81, 82, 83
Volnay 1, 8, 9, 45, 54, 65, 93, 97, 98, 99, 101, 103, 111, 135, 141
Volnay Santenots 99, 141
Vosgros 71
Vosne Romanée 1, 27, 65, 76–8, 141
Vougeot 1, 65, 81, 141

wine and gastronomic fairs 21–5
wine terms 128–31
World War II 16, 48

Yonne, River 1, 20, 70